EPIC SAINTS

EPIC SAINTS

WILD, WONDERFUL, *and* WEIRD
STORIES OF GOD'S HEROES

SHAUN McAFEE

TAN Books
Gastonia, North Carolina

Cover design by Caroline Green

Cover image: St. Columba and the Loch Ness Monster / colour
lithograph / English School, (20th century), © Look and Learn /
Bridgeman Images

Library of Congress Control Number: 2019953846

ISBN: 978-1-5051-1512-3

Published in the United States by
TAN Books
PO Box 269
Gastonia, NC 28053
www.TANBooks.com

Printed in the United States of America

To Gabriel, Tristan, and Dominic—my
wild, wonderful, and weird boys

CONTENTS

INTRODUCTION

By Shaun McAfee

Setting dragons on vocation-deserting novices, blowing up cannons to prove one's worth, and blessing the heck out of church people with beer is not the way we typically think of the saints. We've concocted a picture of saints with lavish prayer lives, patience that outmatches a guardian angel, and enough charity to get them groom-side seats next to Jesus at the heavenly banquet.

But I'm telling you, the saints were wild. They were sometimes rowdy before (and after) they chose God, getting into the thickest of situations. Ever considered dressing up as your persecutor and chewing them out in public? Please meet Eugene Mazenod.

The saints were wonderful. There are saints with gentle names like Thérèse of the Child Jesus, but then there's Christina the Astonishing, who dropped jaws wherever she went with her ridiculous miracles and mind-blowing phenomena.

So the saints did amazing and surprising things, but they

were sometimes just plain weird too. You'd never guess that some saints chose to sleep on the ground, in the rain, with little to nothing on, after walking nearly two thousand kilometers from their hometown, just for a single hour of prayer at a shrine in the middle of nowhere. Or a woman who joined a monastery, living as a monk among religious brothers and priests for almost her entire adult life.

After an intensely intellectual conversion to Catholicism, I'll be honest and say I didn't have a ton of interest in the saints. I heard some great stories in RCIA, but I more enjoyed Augustine's *De Trinitate* or the *Summa Contra Gentiles* of Aquinas before I read Antonio Gallonio's volume on Philip Neri. But when I picked up that world-famous biography and got to the first hilarious story of Neri and the ox, I giggled like a toddler watching the snow peas on *VeggieTales*. As I learned of Neri and his sidesplitting letter to Charles Borromeo, I had to read his life too. And then I discovered that the Lombardian cardinal gave first communion to Aloysius Gonzaga, and that that young man chose Robert Bellarmine as his spiritual director and confessor.

The more I read, the more I wanted to read. And the more I discovered about them, the more I learned about myself, the Church, and most importantly, what God wants of me: continual conversion. St. Neri might have overturned that ox after thinking he was in a rodeo, but that event shaped the mirthful saint. Likewise, I might have dumped a can of paint down the toilet, or traced my whole body on the wall with my mother's lipstick when I was a kid, or shot fireballs at classmates from the Bunsen burner in sixth grade science—or I might not have. It depends on who you ask.

In all seriousness (yes, those things happened), those events shaped me. Those crazy moments and decisions, with the guidance of good mentors and persistent youth pastors, helped me to gain a sense of gratitude for life and the love of others. Now, I can approach my Faith with that same go-big-or-go-home mentality—the same ones that helped Benedict conjure dragons and Boniface to chop down a tree that the pagans thought was their god.

That's why I wanted to write this book. Too often I have the opportunity to tell a good saint story, but I'm guessing everyone already knows. When in reality, they've never even heard of cool saints like Tarcisius. I wanted to compile a list of some of the most outrageous and inspiring saint stories that I and my author-friends have ever heard or read.

But it's far from complete. First of all, there are way too many to tell. We'll have to ask for a sequel! But also, the stories are not all told, yet. The hope, and my personal prayer, is that *you the reader* will become stirred by these of God's heroes in order to have a few saintly stories of your own to share one day. Because the saints aren't just those who have a tapestry hung at the Vatican with forty thousand in attendance for their canonization Mass, but also you and me. Actually, on that note, please stop what you are doing, cross yourself, and pray for me, that I might make it to heaven in one piece.

I'll wait . . .

Now really, please enjoy.

ST. EUGENE DE MAZENOD SCAMS A SCAMMER

By Alex R. Hey

"I am not a bishop to write books," St. Eugène de Mazenod (1782–1861) once said. This summed up his philosophy towards his position as bishop of Marseilles, France. He wanted to be a bishop for the people. As such, his mission was not to preach great sermons or to write great treatises on the Faith; his mission was to serve the people of his diocese.

Mazenod made it a point, then, to be with his people. Despite the administrative duties he had as both a bishop and the leader of a religious order (Oblates of Mary Immaculate), he made a point of administering the sacraments through performing confirmations, numerous and frequent baptisms, tending to the sick, spending hours listening to confessions, and particularly enjoyed the corporeal mercy of reaching out to the poor.

The bishop also had a welcoming office. He set aside a few hours each day for whomever wished to see him. Many people did this, and took their lunches with them to wait in line to see him. Some came to him asking for money, and when this happened, the bishop offered whatever help he could. He wrote of such encounters, "It is nothing to give away money; but to stand there before poor unfortunate people, having done the impossible to help them, and to realize one's powerlessness to do more, that is too much for me." However, this practice of giving money to any person who came to him asking for money was not always treated with respect. On occasion, Mazenod had to endure some rapscallions who tried to scam him, but these miscreants had a hard time pulling a fast one on the wise bishop Eugène.

A well-dressed young man once visited the bishop and began chatting with him. After making small talk for a while, Bishop de Mazenod pressed him for the reason for his visit. The embarrassed young man told him that he was the nephew of another bishop whom he wished to visit but did not have the necessary funds to make the trip. Bishop de Mazenod responded that the young man's uncle was in fact in the building and that he could see him immediately.

The young man made a hasty exit.

The lesson speaks for itself: taking advantage of generosity never ends well.

St. Eugene Mazenod, pray for us.

EXCESSIVE MODESTY OF ST. EUGENE DE MAZENOD

By Alex R. Hey

Eugène de Mazenod was extraordinarily careful to avoid sinning against the virtue of modesty, taking measures to distance himself from the young women he encountered at social engagements and fighting off any advances they made.

While living in Palermo, Italy, this behavior was both the subject of jokes and praise from those at the parties he attended. The people in his social circle were amused by the embarrassment he felt when he was asked to escort a young lady home because she lived near the Mazenod residence. On one happening, he politely refused a request, but the woman insisted. So he awkwardly took her arm and escorted her home.

Eugène was unsure about how he ought to behave in such a situation. He did not want those passing by in carriages to think he was engaging in scandalous activities, so whenever they passed by, he made the young girl step aside into bushes or whatever shadows were nearby to hide from the lights of the carriage.

The young girl was so struck by this behavior that she could not help but tell others about it. Eugène's father, upon hearing the story, chided him for using excessive modesty. It's not wrong to also feel sad for the lady who just needed an escort home! But everyone could agree the principles that inspired his actions were in the right place. Young men today could take a few pages from his playbook.

St. Eugene Mazenod, pray for us.

ST. BONIFACE THE LUMBERJACK

By Alex R. Hey

As a measure of his extensive missionary travels, Boniface (675–754) knew that in winter, the inhabitants of the village of Geismar, which is in Germany, gathered around a huge old oak tree known as the "Thunder Oak," dedicated to the pagan god Thor (not the superhero). During this annual event, the locals would offer a human sacrifice, usually a small child, to the pagan god.

Boniface desired their conversion but also for the needless deaths of children to end. To prove to the people living there that the Christian God is more powerful than the pagan Thor, and to end superstitious practices involving the tree, Boniface decided to take action and just chop the doggone thing down.

On the night of Christmas Eve, his companion missionaries were somewhat afraid upon reaching the town, but

Boniface encouraged them, "Here is the Thunder Oak; and here the cross of Christ shall break the hammer of the false god Thor." Arriving at the time of the sacrifice, which was interrupted by their presence, Boniface grabbed an ax and chopped down the Thunder Oak of mighty Thor. The bishop then preached the Gospel to the people, using the image of a little fir tree behind the destroyed tree. Tradition says that he preached a simple sermon they could understand: "This little tree, is as a Christ-child; gather about it, not in the wild wood, but in your own homes; there it will shelter no deeds of blood, but loving gifts and rites of kindness." Awed by the destruction of the oak tree, and heeding Boniface's preaching, the inhabitants of Geismer were baptized.

Another story states that St. Boniface took the wood from the giant oak tree and built a chapel dedicated to St. Peter. Whatever the ending, the fact remains that St. Boniface is largely responsible for the conversion of the Germanic people and is rightfully their patron. Saintly courage comes in many forms; be prepared to preach the Gospel in the form which God is preparing you.

St. Boniface, pray for us.

HAVE SAINTS ALWAYS BEEN CANONIZED THE SAME WAY?

By Shaun McAfee

The quick answer to this question is a big fat no. The idea and process of canonization is one that has evolved or, as I like to say, matured throughout the history of the Church.

The idea of canonizing a thing in the Church comes from the Greek word *kanon*, which was first used to denote a straight rod and was later used to mean a measuring stick, denoting a rule or a norm.

The Church has always had saints, but it is that norm of recognizing an individual as a saint that has matured since the infancy days of the Church. Early on, few rules, strictly speaking, were created. Not to mention, the Church was small and bishops, though in communion with Rome, did enjoy some liberty in the regulation of saints and what we call their *cultus*, or their following and cause. In those times, and for centuries, placing the remains in a church (usually just the bones of a martyr) was enough to recognize them as the patron and saint. But gradually, as early as the eighth and ninth centuries, as the persecutions generally died down and the Church became more complex administratively, appeals to the pope for recognition of a saint's life were made.

According to some historical sources, the first saint to be officially canonized by a pope was St. Ulrich in 973, bishop of Augsburg, by Pope John XV at the Lateran Council of 993. Pope Alexander III (1159–1181) began to reserve the cases of canonization to the Holy See, and this became general law under Gregory IX (1227–1241).

Several centuries later, Pope Sixtus V (1585–1590) obligated the Congregation of Rites, part of the Roman Curia, the duty of managing the processes of beatification and canonization. Following this, Pope Urban VIII banned the communal cult of any person not as yet beatified or canonized by the Church. An exception was granted for those whose cult persisted from time immemorial or for at least one hundred years.

These laws of Pope Urban VIII, together with later legislation constructed by Pope Benedict XIV, formed the basis of the procedures for beatification and canonization found in the Code of Canon Law, promulgated in 1917, of the Roman Catholic Church.

The Church has always had saints, but the process of recognizing their individual cults has matured to introduce normalization and unity in the procedure.

THEY MIGHT NOT KNOW WHAT THEY DO, BUT WE DO: ST. MOSES THE BLACK

By Alex R. Hey

Saint Moses the Black, a native of Ethiopia, was born in the fourth century. He managed to escape slavery when his master, an Egyptian official, discovered his involvement in plots of theft and murder. He later became the leader of a gang of seventy-five robbers. He and his gang spread terror throughout the Nile Valley.

While on the run from the authorities, he took shelter with some monks in the desert. After observing their daily routine, he was proverbially smacked straight by their peaceful and prayerful lifestyle. Their daily activities inspired him to convert to Christianity and become a monk with them.

Days later, Moses was in his cell and was attacked by a group of robbers. He defended himself and single-handedly subdued the men without unnecessary suffering. Then, he dragged them into the chapel where the other monks were praying. Stating, in our words, that he did not believe it to be Christian to beat the snot out of them, he asked the monks what he should do with them. The robbers were overwhelmed, as he was months prior, and converted to Christianity.

Moses the Black, under the tutelage of St. Isidore, overcame his violent past and became a great saint of the Church. This puts him in the same category with the likes of Augustine, Francis of Assisi, and many others who overcame their sketchy pasts to live a life of heroic virtue. On the cross, Jesus prayed, "Father, forgive them; for they know not what they do" (Lk 23:34). Oftentimes, it is those Christians who have dabbled in sin that know very well the chains and prison created by them. When we take action to encourage and help others who engage in the sins that they know not, but we do, we make a tremendous act of mercy.

St. Moses the Black, pray for us.

PATRON OF MAN'S BEST FRIEND: ST. ROCH

By Alex R. Hey

After losing his parents at the age of twenty, St. Roch (1295–1327) sold all of his possessions and traveled to Rome. There, he began caring for plague victims, miraculously curing some of the patients by touching them or by making the Sign of the Cross. He would soon contract the plague.

When he realized this, Roch ran off to the woods to die. To his shock, a hunting dog brought him food and began licking his wounds. The wounds miraculously healed, and a spring of clean water sprung out from the ground where he lay, providing him with a constant supply of clear and drinkable water, a rarity at this time in Rome.

Following his recovery, he returned to his home town of Montpellier. Unfortunately, he was not recognized by his uncle. He was accused of being a spy and thrown in jail. Instead of claiming his rightful place in Montpellier, he told no one of his true identity. For the next five years, Roch lived in prison being cared for by an angel until he died in the year

1327. It was only after his death that people realized who he was by the birthmark on his chest.

The Fathers of the Council of Constance in 1414 ordered public prayers and processions asking for the intercession of St. Roch. His intercession worked, and the plague in Constance that was ravaging the city at the time ended. St. Roch is the patron saint of the plague, cholera, skin rashes, dogs, and several cities and towns of Italy. His life reminds us that suffering and denial are part of the Christian life. More deeply, sometimes this suffering demands our silence in the face of those offering us a superficial mercy or justice because God is the ultimate guarantor of mercy and justice. Jesus demonstrated this perfectly in the presence of Pilate. "Now Jesus stood before the governor; and the governor asked him, 'Are you the King of the Jews?' Jesus said to him, 'You have said so.' But when he was accused by the chief priests and elders, he made no answer. Then Pilate said to him, 'Do you not hear how many things they testify against you?' But he gave him no answer, not even to a single charge; so that the governor wondered greatly" (Mt 27:11–14).

St. Roch, pray for us.

ST. COLUMBA AND THE LOCH NESS MONSTER

By Alex R. Hey

The *Vita Columbae* (La. "Life of Columba") is the source for most of what we know about the life of St. Columba (521–597). This biography was written by Adomnán a hundred years following the death of Columba. Adomnán was the ninth abbot of Iona, a monastic community founded by Columba. In Book Two of the Vita, Adomnán tells of an incident that occurred on the shores of Loch Ness.

The story goes that Columba came across a group of Picts. These people are now world-renowned for their "standing stones" of northeastern Scotland, made for their devotions to their polytheistic gods. When Columba approached the Picts, they were burying a man who had been killed by a creature living in the waters nearby.

As "Nessie" began to set his sights on another swimmer in the water, Columba made the Sign of the Cross and said,

"Thou shalt go no further, nor touch the man; go back with all speed." The beast fled; the native people were amazed and began to admire the God of the Christians. Traditional stories also say that St. Columba laid his staff on the dead man's chest and brought him back to life. History relates that Saints Patrick, Brigid of Kildare, Ninan, and Columba converted many Pictish tribes. Fiction or not, it is not impossible and it is an amusing tale. Nothing is impossible with God.

St. Columba, pray for us.

ST. MARGARET CLITHEROW REFUSES TO PLEAD

By Alex R. Hey

A lthough all Catholics were under persecution in England in the late sixteenth century, it was the priests who were brutally martyred for continuing in their Catholic Faith. St. Margaret Clitherow (1556–1586), mother of three, offered shelter to priests who were trying to secretly carry out their priestly duties. However, her clandestine activities were discovered, and following a raid on her home on March 12, 1586, she was arrested and brought to trial two days later on the charges of hearing Mass and "such like." It was not her first time to jail, though, and her wealthy husband continually paid her fines for not attending non-Catholic services. With familiarity and trust in God, she entered court to defend herself against the charges.

In response to hearing the charges in court, Margaret Clitherow replied that she had never harbored enemies of the queen. Then, when asked how she wanted to be tried, she replied, "Having made no offense, I need no trial," instead of the standard "By God and the country."

After pressing her for a plea, her only response was, "If you say that I have offended and must be tried, I will be tried by none but God and your own consciences."

The courts deliberated and sometime later, they brought out "two lewd fellows" wearing vestments found at her house during the raid. She was asked if she liked the vestments, and she responded, "I like them well if they are on the backs of those who know how to use them for God's honor, as they were made." Anxious, their next ploy was to claim she did not harbor priests for religious reasons but for "harlotries."

The next day, she was brought back to court where she was once again encouraged to plead. She held firm stating, "I think you have no witness against me but only children which with an apple and a rod you may make to say what you will." After one of the judges snapped and described the brutal death she would endure if she continued to refuse to plead, she stated, "If this judgement be according to your conscience, I pray God to send you a better judgement before him. I thank you heartily for this."

At this point, she also knew that if she entered into a plea or any other sort of trial, her three children would have been forced to testify; the apparent motives behind her bold words. If her children were to cause any doubt about their testimony, it was standard to torture them.

Sadly, St. Margaret Clitherow never got a better judgement. She was martyred, while pregnant with her fourth child, on March 25, 1586 by a method of execution known as "pressing." This was the standard form of death for those failing to enter into a plea.

It was reported that the two sergeants who were ordered to carry out the execution had hired four beggars to do it instead. They stripped her, had a handkerchief tied across her face, and finally laid a sharp rock the size of a man's fist on her spine. The men took the door from her own house and placed it on top of her, loading it with an immense weight of rocks and stones until the sharp rock would break her back. Margaret remained silent. She endured fifteen minutes of unspeakable pain before she died, but her body was left for six hours before the weight was removed.

Clitherow not only refused to renounce her Faith, she was shrewd to respond to her accusers with answers that would protect the needless suffering of her children, offering her incredible suffering as a witness to them, to the priests she harbored, and to us.

St. Margaret Clitherow, pray for us.

BLESSED MIGUEL PRO: MASTER OF DISGUISE

By Alex R. Hey

In the early twentieth century, the Mexican government turned against the Catholic Church. The Church was forced to operate underground. But one Jesuit priest, Miguel Pro (1891–1927), was especially adept at ministering to this underground Church.

Despite being wanted (and hunted) by the police, Blessed Miguel Pro went to great lengths to carry out his ministry. He owned a policeman costume and used it to casually walk into police stations to bring the Eucharist to imprisoned Catholics being held in jail. This uniform proved to be especially handy on the day one of the houses in which he had been secretly celebrating Mass was raided by the police just after Mass ended.

Before the house was completely surrounded, Pro snuck out of a side door and escaped to a nearby safe house. Then,

because he had a good sense of humor and was quite auda-
cious, he changed into his police costume, went back to the
house from which had just escaped, and chewed out the
policemen that were looking for him for not apprehending
him.

Besides his police uniform, Miguel Pro had a number of
costumes he used to sneak about to baptize infants, hear
confessions, distribute Communion, and to perform wed-
dings. He owned costumes that allowed him to appear as a
beggar, a street sweeper, chauffeur, garage mechanic, farm
laborer, and a playboy. Yes, you read that right—a playboy—
true story.

Once, while his taxi cab was being pursued by several
police cars, Pro ordered his cab to slow down as it rounded a
corner. He rolled out, lit a cigar, and took a young, attractive
woman by the arm. The police cars roared past, paying no
attention to what appeared to them as a couple of love birds
but was actually a fugitive Jesuit priest.

Blessed Miguel Pro, pray for us.

THREE ST. ARNOLDS
AND THE BEER-ACLES

By Sarah Spittler

Jesus's miracle of turning water into wine set an important precedent for Christ-followers everywhere: a little fun never killed nobody. Catholics continue to celebrate Mass with real wine and even received special exemption to do so during the prohibition era in the United States.

Throughout history, many monasteries and abbeys have produced their wine and beer. This practice dates back to the Middle Ages, and with it, there are stories of saints performing miraculous acts regarding alcoholic beverages. In fact, three different St. Arnolds have miracles surrounding beer attributed to them. The hoppy situations surrounding them are a bit cloudy—the same miracles (or beer-acles, as we joyfully annotate) and stories may have any one of them named as the presider, depending on the source. The best estimate relates St. Arnold of Soissons as the patron saint of hop pickers, St. Arnold of Metz as the patron saint of brewers, and St. Arnold of Oudenaarde as the founder of the Abbey of St. Peter in Oudenburg.

The patron saint of hop pickers, St. Arnold of Soissons, was a monk in Oudenburg, Belgium during the eleventh century. The main beer-acle associated with St. Arnold of Soissons followed the collapse of an abbey brewery in Flanders. The destruction, of course, diminished the abbey's supply of the beverage, causing St. Arnold to pray for an increase in the froth and foam. Miraculously, his prayers worked! The stores of beer previously damaged were amply replenished, and those who lived in the local village clamored to canonize him immediately. His preaching to the hop-growing region of Brabant in Belgium had made him popular with the townspeople, and between his own congregation and those to whom he preached, Arnold's cause for sainthood was well-developed before his death.

Arnold of Soissons and Arnold of Oudenaarde are most often mixed up, and for good reason. Both Arnolds were preachers in the eleventh century in Flanders, Belgium. Both are considered patrons of Belgian brewing and promoted the consumption of beer for good health. One distinguishing factor draws from the legend of St. Arnold of Oudenaarde beginning his ministry on the battlefield. While serving in the military, St. Arnold called upon the Lord to provide restoration to his injured and sickly friends. Through this intercession, Arnold was able to conjure up mugs full of beer to strengthen the soldiers in need. He later went on to become a Benedictine monk and study the art of brewing.

The most information can be found regarding St. Arnold

of Metz, who is celebrated yearly in Belgium on the "Day of Bier." Being a man of the early seventh century France, Arnold deeply believed in the healing power of beer. He received his patron-saint-of-brewers status after saving many of the inhabitants of the local community from the disease. St. Arnold encouraged those who lived around his abbey to drink beer, especially the beer brewed at the abbey, rather than water. He claimed beer had a special "gift of health" surpassing that of water. Unknown to practitioners of medicine and hygiene at the time, many of the pathogens causing the outbreak of the plague were transmitted through local water sources. To save his companions from the plague, St. Arnold reportedly dunked his crucifix into a brew kettle at the abbey, asking people to drink the beer only from that particular kettle. To top it off, St. Arnold of Metz informed his followers, "For man's sweat and God's love, beer came into the world."

Saints Arnold, Arnold, and Arnold, pray for us.

"WHICH CROSS IS MINE?" ST. THOMAS KOZAKI AND COMPANIONS

By Jessica McAfee

February 5, 1597, fourteen-year-old Thomas Kozaki, his father, and twenty-six others were crucified and pierced with spears after an excruciating journey to their deaths, marched from city to city, collecting the jailed "Kakure Kirishitans" with little food, water, and clothes to protect them through the arduous journey. Because they refused to renounce their Catholic faith and apostatize, they were marched to Nashizaka Hill where all of Nagasaki could watch.

They were to be the first of thousands who were killed for the Faith in this location, and their faithfulness begat faith in others even as they marched from Kyoto to Nagasaki, which took them a month on foot. Seventeen days before, on the

way to Nagasaki, St. Thomas Kozaki wrote the following letter to his mother.

> With the help of the Lord's grace I am writing these
> lines. The priests and the others who are journeying
> to be crucified in Nagasaki in all number twenty-four,
> as testified in the sentience that is carried on a board
> ahead of us.
>
> You should not worry about me and my father
> Michael. I hope to see you both very soon, there in
> paradise. Although you need the priests, if you are
> deeply sorry for your sins and have much devotion
> in the hour of your death, and you remember and
> acknowledge the many blessings of Jesus Christ, then
> you will be saved.
>
> And bear in mind that everyone in this world has
> come to an end, and so strive that you will not lose
> the happiness of heaven. Whatever men may impose
> on you, try to have patience and show much charity
> for everyone.
>
> It is really necessary that my two brothers, Mancius
> and Philip, do not fall into the hands of heathens. I
> commend you to Our Lord, and I send you prayers
> for everyone we know. Remember to have great sorrow
> for your sins, for this alone is important. Although he
> sinned against God, Adam was saved by his sorrow
> and penance.

During their journey, they were voluntarily joined by
two more, making the number of total martyrs twenty-six,

instead of the twenty-four as noted in St. Thomas's letter. Of those to be martyred were three young boys who were altar servers. The youngest was nine.

In the hour of their crucifixion, they were offered, one last time, their freedom if they would apostatize. One of the altar servers replied with a heroic, "Sir, it would be better if you yourself became a Christian and could go to heaven where I am going. So which cross is mine?" It was noted that there was a beautiful peace and calmness surrounding especially the altar servers who were killed for their faith on that day.

St. Thomas Kozaki and companions, pray for us.

A FAMILY THAT PRAYS TOGETHER: ST. ZOE OF PAMPHYLIA

By Theresa Zoe Williams

St. Zoe of Pamphylia (d. 286) and her family—several of whom are also saints—were born as Christian slaves to a pagan ruler named Catullus (not the Latin poet). On the occasion of the birth of their master's son, food was sent to all of his slaves that had obediently offered sacrifices according to the pagan norms, as directed. St. Zoe and her family, though, refused to eat the food, going so far as to pour the wine out on the ground and to throw the meat to the dogs.

When he saw the family do this, he became enraged, ordering them to be tortured, starting with St. Zoe's two sons. As they were being tortured, Zoe and her husband, Nicostratus, counseled their sons to persevere, and the sons then encouraged their parents to remain faithful despite what might happen. As ordered, the soldiers then brutally tortured Zoe and Nicostratus.

They were given the opportunity to be spared further pain and possibly death if they were to renounce their faith. But they were unrelenting in their perseverance and all four were thrown into a furnace where they all perished.

Although they died, miraculously, their bodies were untouched by the flames. Their bodies were free of any mark of the flames, and it was reported that an angelic choir could be heard amid the fire.

It is said that the family who prays together, stays together. And they did.

St. Zoe, pray for us.

ST. TERESA MARGARET REDI AND HER UN-DECOMPOSING BODY

By Theresa Zoe Williams

Anna Maria Redi (1774–1770) became a Discalced Carmelite nun and lived in Florence. Anna would later take the name Teresa Margaret. Teresa was only twenty-three years old when she died and has been called a victim of the fire of Divine Love. She lived an extraordinary and hidden life of holiness and went from perfect health to her grave in a very short amount of time. Investigators have speculated that the cause of death was a strangulated hernia. She lived a quiet life, but the most miraculous part of St. Teresa Margaret's earthly tenure was what happened to her body after her death.

When St. Teresa Margaret died, her body had become quite bloated and disfigured from disease—so badly, in fact, that the nuns considered not having a public viewing for fear of just how poorly she looked. The saint's hands and feet were almost black and she seemed to be decomposing right in front of their eyes! Because of this, the nuns made swift preparations for her funeral and burial.

Suddenly, though, the discoloration in St. Teresa Margaret's face was much less pronounced, almost as though the decomposition was reversing. The nuns reversed their plans and the burial was postponed. Another examination a few hours later revealed that the nun's face, hands, and feet had all regained their natural coloring, and the burial was again postponed for yet another day.

Fifty-two hours after her death, St. Teresa Margaret's skin had returned to its natural, life-like tint and her once rigid limbs became flexible and easily moved. Some remarked that she looked so beautiful and so peaceful that she seemed only to be sleeping, with no evidence of bodily corruption or decay. The archbishop even remarked that she had no odor of decay but rather had that of a sweet fragrance of roses, which he called "the odor of sanctity." St. Teresa Margaret Redi of the Sacred Heart's body remains incorrupt to this day and lies in the Discalced Carmelite Monastery of St. Teresa on Via dei Bruni in Florence, Italy.

Where there is holiness, there is also purity of body, the temple.

St. Teresa Margaret Redi of the Sacred Heart, pray for us.

ST. ISIDORE BAKANJA: CATECHIST MARTYR OF THE SCAPULAR

By Theresa Zoe Williams

Isidore Bakanja (1887–1909) was born in the Ziare (present-day Congo) when many Belgians companies arrived to take advantage of the region's rich deposits of rubber and ivory. Unfortunately, they greatly mistreated their workers and the Belgian government denounced the misconduct. Pope Leo XIII sent Trappist missionaries there at the petition of the Belgian government.

When he was an early teen, Isidore was baptized after obtaining work as an assistant mason constructing buildings for the Belgian colonizers. The missionaries stressed two devotions: the Rosary and the scapular. At his baptism, Isidore's name was inscribed both in the parish baptismal registry and in that of the Scapular Confraternity. He so

loved both the Rosary and the scapular that he would never
be without them or parted from them.

He preached the Catholic faith to anyone who would
listen and then would instruct new believers in the Faith.
Bakanja followed a trusted employer to a new job in a region
that was very unfriendly towards people from his region and
to Christians, but Isidore accompanied him anyway, wish-
ing that all might be brought to Christ. The supervisor at
the new plantation, known as Longange, was particularly
anti-Christian and often tormented Isidore for his faith.
Longange demanded that Isidore stop teaching the Faith
and stop teaching natives how to pray, but Isidore refused.
Longange also tormented him for praying his rosary and
demanded that the rosary never be brought into his presence
again; Isidore still was undeterred in his devotion.

When Isidore realized just how much Longange hated
him, he asked for a letter releasing him so he could return
to his village, but Longange refused. He sarcastically told
Isidore that he should ask his God for the letter.

One night at supper, Longange saw the scapular around
Isidore's neck and demanded that he take it off; Isidore did
not. A few days later, Longange again saw the scapular and
flew into a rage, demanding that Isidore be beaten with
twenty-five strokes. Despite the suffering, Isidore refused to
discard his rosary and scapular and also continued to cate-
chize the others.

Days later, Longange saw Isidore saying his prayers while
walking to the marsh. Longange confronted him and told
him to lie down for a whipping. Bakanja countered that he

had never stolen from Longange, that he never went near his wife, and that he was innocent of all things.

Furious, Longange called for his chief disciplinarian to whip Isidore with an elephant hide whip that had two nails protruding from its end. Longange then ripped the scapular from Isidore's neck and threw it to the dogs who ran off with it. The beating began with two servants holding his arms and legs down. If Isidore expressed pain, Longange kicked him repeatedly. Isidore let the master know he was dying, but the beating continued and did not stop until the torturer was so fatigued that he could no longer use the whip. Testimony survives that estimates a sustained 200 to 250 blows, mostly to his back.

The young man attempted to rise from his pool of blood, murmuring "[This] man has killed me with his whip. He did not want me to pray to God. He killed me because I said my prayers. I stole nothing from him. It's because I was praying to God." Longange had Isidore chained by the feet in a room where rubber was processed, hoping he would die in isolation and that his death would not be reported to the authorities. But a few days later, the company's inspector visited and found Isidore. Horrified, the inspector turned Longange in and he was later condemned by the courts.

Bakanja was taken back to his village where he died six months later from his wounded and weakened state. The priest there tried to offer consolations to Isidore, but he would reply, "It's nothing if I die. If God wants me to live, I'll live! If God wants me to die, I'll die. It's all the same to me." He stated that he was not angry with his master and that he would pray for him, especially in heaven. Until his very last breath, St. Isidore prayed fervently, always prayed the Rosary, and was never again separated from his scapular. He was fourteen years old.

We are commanded of this: to pray for our persecutors.

St. Isidore Bakhita, pray for us.

ST. NICHOLAS OF TOLENTINO AND THE POOR SOULS IN PURGATORY

By Theresa Zoe Williams

Nicholas of Tolentino (1246–1305) was an Italian priest of the Augustinian order. Becoming a monk and then a priest by the time he was twenty-five years old, he was known for excellent preaching and mystical gifts. In a vision, angels recited the town name of Tolentino to him, and so he made the decision to move there permanently with the order.

One day, he was given a vision of a brother Augustinian priest who had just died, Father Pellegrino of Osimo. Father Pellegrino came and told Nicholas about the sufferings he and the other souls in purgatory endured and proceeded to beg Nicholas to offer Masses for them so that they might find peace.

Nicholas went straight to his superior with this vision and was granted permission to offer Requiem Masses every day for the next week for the souls in purgatory. In addition to this, Nicholas also offered his Divine Office and all his other prayers for the relief of those poor souls in purgatory.

At the end of the week, Father Pellegrino again appeared to Nicholas, leading a host of souls, all of them dressed in dazzling white robes. They thanked the priest for his fervent prayers and told him that because of those prayers, they had been released from purgatory. Then, they left his vision as they were taken into heaven, shrouded in glorious light.

St. Nicholas of Tolentino was later named patron of the poor souls in purgatory for his devotion to prayer and sacrifice for them. The Church teaches: "From the beginning the Church has honored the memory of the dead and offered prayer in suffrage for them, above all the Eucharistic sacrifice, so that, this purified, they may attain the beatific vision of God" (CCC 1032).

We should always ask for Masses for the dead to be said and offer our Rosaries as petitions to free the souls in purgatory. Would we not ask for the same when we die?

St. Nicholas of Tolentino, pray for us.

WHAT IS THE GENERAL ROMAN CALENDAR?

By Shaun McAfee

Sometimes, Catholics aren't completely sure what the Roman Calendar is, even though it's a critical component of the Catholic life. Really, as a frame of reference, *it is the Catholic life.*

To be straightforward, the General Roman Calendar is the liturgical calendar that indicates the dates of celebrations of saints and mysteries of our Faith in the Roman Rite. The *Catechism of the Catholic Church* explains, "Through this annual cycle the liturgy unfolds the whole mystery of Christ from the Incarnation and Nativity to the Ascension, to Pentecost and the hope of the coming of the Lord" (CCC 1163).

In other words, this calendar lays out all of the feast days, memorials, solemnities, and other days of celebration for our worship. It sets the entire Roman Church in sync with the same schedule of worship. *Sacrosanctum Concilium* says,

"Holy Mother Church is conscious that she must celebrate the saving work of her divine Spouse by devoutly recalling it on certain days throughout the course of the year. Every week, on the day which she has called the Lord's day, she keeps the memory of the Lord's resurrection, which she also celebrates once in the year, together with His blessed passion, in the most solemn festival of Easter."[1]

During the liturgical year, we also discover the great heroes of our Faith in order to better fill us with hope and endurance to live out our Catholic lives with love and service. As we take up participation with the Church in celebrating their lives, we proclaim the achievement of Christ, and by observing their examples, we may become strengthened in our faith in Christ and our participation in his suffering. The *Constitution on Sacred Liturgy* puts it this way: "By celebrating the passage of these saints from earth to heaven the Church proclaims the paschal mystery achieved in the saints who have suffered and been glorified with Christ; she proposes them to the faithful as examples drawing all to the Father through Christ, and through their merits she pleads for God's favors."[2]

The Roman Calendar is a true gift to the faithful: lighting our path to true unity in the Universal Church and communion with our Lord by reflecting on his life and offering us the opportunity to participate in works of mercy.

---

[1]   *Sacrosanctum Concilium*, 102.
[2]   Ibid., 104.

ST. FRANCIS XAVIER AND THE NOT-EXACTLY-A-SECRET WEAPON

By Theresa Zoe Williams

Francisco de Jasso y Azpilicueta was born in the Kingdom of Navarre (present-day Spain) and became a priest, taking the name Francis Xavier (1506–1552), and later co-founded the Society of Jesus, known as the Jesuits. He led some of the most extensive missionary work in the history of the Church and was influential in the evangelization of India and Eastern Asia.

While Francis Xavier was in India in the Cape of Comorin, there one day fell an unrest upon the village. He was on his way to make a sick call when the scream of a woman pierced through the village. Francis stopped dead in his tracks. Merchants on the street stopped bargaining, children stopped playing, everyone became still.

Then, two women suddenly appeared bounding down the street in such a way that Francis at first thought they were drunk. But he quickly noticed blood gushing from one of their shoulders and the other woman fell to the ground. St. Francis rushed to the women and, to his horror, saw that they were mortally wounded. Unimaginably, one was pregnant and sustained such a deep slash across her abdomen that Francis believed he could see the baby inside. The woman he was holding started screaming, "Vadagars! Vadagars!" who were especially vicious Muslim raiders.

The villagers started running for cover and the woman St. Francis was holding was shot in the neck with an arrow while another arrow landed right at his feet. St. Francis Xavier stood up quickly, wheeled around to face the oncoming horde of attackers, and roared, "IN THE NAME OF CHRIST!"

Though he was but one unarmed man against a horde on horseback, he drew out a spiritual weapon, prepared to defend his people, a black, six-inch crucifix, and he raised it high in the air.

In that moment, to the raiders, Xavier appeared to be gigantic and his eyes appeared to burn like the sun. The raiders, completely terrified, instantly reared their horses and turned around in such a fright and tumult that a cloud of dust enveloped them as they left.

After a few moments, the hoofbeats could be heard no more and Francis Xavier lowered the crucifix and placed it lovingly back in his robes. Christ, the weapon against all danger, had protected his people from terrible death and destruction through the courage of his faithful servant.

In the face of persecution, we must still wield our spiritual armor and weaponry.

St. Francis Xavier, pray for us.

ST. FRANCIS XAVIER LEARNS AN IMPORTANT LESSON ABOUT CRABS AND CROSSES

By Theresa Zoe Williams

Miracles aren't always pretty. Sometimes, they're downright hilarious.

Once while sailing to the island of Malacca in Indonesia, Francis Xavier and his companions ran into a terrible storm and their ship, called a carracca and more like a large boat, was ill-equipped to handle such an event.

The companions of Francis thought all was lost, but the holy missionary had no such fear. He stepped to the bow, removed the beloved crucifix which he always wore at his breast, and chucked it into the ocean. The storm immediately ceased and the waters again became calm.

44

And then he realized he threw his crucifix into the ocean. He waited, but it did not return to him. This crucifix was the central object of other miracles—surely it would float, or something, for him to retrieve it. But nope. It was gone for sure, as he watched it fade into the deep blue and out of sight. Francis Xavier was brokenhearted over his loss.

After a day of sailing, the missionaries reached their destination and the sea had once again become rough, though not enough to put them in real danger. Francis Xavier and his companion Faustus Rodriguez hopped out of the boat and walked a short distance along the shoreline.

Something suddenly caught their eye: a crab with the mark of a cross on its back. Xavier immediately thought of his beloved cross; he might have even felt humiliated—like a twisted joke.

"How—but, whe—no!" must have been his only thoughts when he looked at the claws of the creature, which was actually holding *his crucifix.*

With their jaws probably on the ground, the two watched as the crab walked right to them, carrying the crucifix upright in its claws, turned to Francis and remained quiet and calm while Francis then knelt down, took it, and thanked the creature.

Then the crab said nothing, turned around, and returned to the sea—crabs don't usually talk but if it were Francis of Assisi, maybe this story would be different. Francis tenderly embraced and kissed his crucifix and returned it around his neck at his breast. Then he and his companion remained at that site for a half hour, giving praise and thanksgiving to

God for returning the saint's treasure before they continued on their journey.

That species of crab still exists. Its nomenclature is *charybdis feriatus* and it is indigenous to the ocean around Malacca. It was no mistake that God, from the beginning of creation, planned this great moment for the building of faith.

It's easy to grow attached, personally, to our sacramentals, but we should remember always that they are tools to build the Faith.

St. Francis Xavier, pray for us.

CAN YOU REALLY TRUST A WOLF? ST. EDMUND THE MARTYR

By Theresa Zoe Williams

There seems to be a patron of nearly everything, especially animals. Even animals we—well . . . the ones we'd rather not encounter. Like wolves.

Edmund was the English king of East Anglia (841–869) who led his army against a Viking horde that had invaded his realm in November of 869. The invaders were led by Ivar the Boneless and his brother Ubba, sons of the legendary Norse hero and king of Denmark Ragnar Lothbrok. Unfortunately, the Vikings scattered the English troops and took Edmund hostage. Not the hopeful start to the conflict he wanted.

Ivar, the Viking chief, promised to spare Edmund's life if he would renounce the Christian faith and swear fealty to the Vikings. Edmund resolutely refused. Enraged, Ivar then had Edmund tied to a nearby tree and shot through with arrows. When they were sure Edmund was dead, the Vikings cut off his head and threw it deep into the snowy forest.

Later, some of the Englishmen ventured out to the site to collect Edmund's body for burial. His corpse was easily found right by the tree where he was killed, but they were distressed that they could not locate the holy man's head.

Like a dream, they heard a voice calling, "Here! Here!" The language was not English but Latin and did not sound like a human's voice. So they cautiously followed the voice into the woods, and there they found a wolf lying on the ground, gently caressing St. Edmund's head with his paws.

The wolf let the Englishmen take the head upon his escort of the group back to their village. Once St. Edmund's body and head were safe, the wolf returned to the forest. Because of this wolf's devotion and reverence toward the holy man, St. Edmund was named the patron saint of wolves.

All creation proclaims his glory. Even wolves.

St. Edmund the Martyr, pray for us.

ST. CLARE AND THE SARACENS

By Theresa Zoe Williams

Frederick II was one of the most successful rulers of the Holy Roman Empire, inheriting kingship of Germany and going on to conquer Italy, Burgundy, and Jerusalem. He was excommunicated four separate times and never enjoyed a time not in conflict with the bishops of Rome.

It turns out that Frederick was born in Assisi, Italy, in the same year and the birthplace of another influential person: St. Clare of Assisi (1194–1253). In time, she would out-conquer Frederick, in the form hearts. But first, she would defeat his soldiers too.

Now, when Clare was quite sick, the schismatic Fredrick II set his sights on conquering Italy and had an army of twenty thousand well-trained Saracens at his disposal. To accomplish this, he needed to take the influential Umbrian city of Assisi. He chose his Saracen army for the task in the year 1224.

As the Saracens began to advance, word spread throughout Assisi of their impending arrival, so all of the people, even from throughout the countryside, were brought into the city for protection and the great gates of the city were securely shut. Only Clare and her Poor Ladies remained outside the walls inside of their little convent, defenseless. Of course, the Saracens would have to march right past the convent on their way to the city walls! The Poor Ladies prayed with fasting.

When the Saracens arrived, Clare was quite ill in and was resigned to her bed. The Saracens intended to show no mercy to the cloistered sisters and began banging on the doors.

Clare, hearing the racket, sat up a little and asked what all the commotion was. "It's the Saracens!" the little sisters told her, in terrified voices.

With great effort, Clare pulled herself out of bed, much to the dismay of the sisters, and asked for the silver and ivory monstrance holding the Blessed Sacrament to be brought to her. Taking this in her hands, she walked to a large window that overlooked the square, and there she presented Jesus in the Eucharist to this army of infidels. Crying out, St. Clare prayed, "I ask you, O my Lord, that it might please you not to let these poor servants of yours fall into the hands of cruel infidels and pagans. I ask you, O my Lord, that you would also watch over this town and all those good people, who, for the love of you, help us and provide our necessities."

And from the monstrance came forth a sweet voice:

"Because of your love, I will watch over you and them always."

After hearing this, the Saracens began to scatter on the hillside. The scouts at Assisi were watching from far off, but when morning came without shouts of war, the gates of the city were thrown open and the people came and went again in peace. Clare had saved the city by the presentation of Jesus Christ in the Blessed Sacrament!

Never underestimate the power of the Real Presence.

St. Clare of Assisi, pray for us.

IGNORING PARENTAL ADVISORIES: ST. ANNA WANG

By Theresa Zoe Williams

The Boxer Rebellion was an anti-imperialist, anti-colo-
nial, and especially anti-Christian uprising in China
that took place between 1899 and 1901. All Christians,
evangelical Protestants and Catholics, died together. But the
clergy and Catholic laity suffered catastrophic numbers: close
to fifty priests and religious were killed for not renouncing
the Faith, and over thirty thousand Chinese Catholics were
slain for refusing to apostatize. Anna Wang (1886–1900)
was caught up in the movement.

She was the daughter of Christian parents, though her
mother had died when she was younger; her step-mother
was also a Christian. Anna was born in Majiazhuang in
1886 and it was there that she and her family, among other

Chinese Christians, were captured by the Boxers on July 21, 1900. The Christians were given the martyr's ultimatum: renounce the Faith or die.

All of Anna's family renounced their faith and walked through a door to safety. Anna's step-mother tried to drag her through the door with her but Anna remained resolute and fought back, telling her, "I believe in God. I am a Christian. I do not renounce God. Jesus, save me!"

That night, Anna led the remaining group of Christians in a vigil of prayer until they were led to their executions the next morning. She led the group in prayer and an Act of Contrition on their way to the execution site.

When they arrived, Anna knelt down facing the village church and prayed loudly. Once again, her executioner gave her the chance to renounce her faith and save her life, but she did not hear him the first time because she was so enrapt in prayer. He touched her forehead to gain her attention, which greatly startled her. Regaining her composure, she stated, "I prefer to die rather than give up my faith."

Greatly angered, the executioner cut off part of her left shoulder and asked her again if she would leave the Church, to which she simply replied, "No." Then the executioner cut off her entire left arm.

Still kneeling, Anna raised her right hand to heaven and said, "The door of heaven is open." Then she whispered the name of Jesus three times, lowered her head, and was decapitated.

The challenge of the Gospel is that, despite the circumstances, we have to choose God no matter the cost.

St. Anna Wang and Holy Chinese Martyrs, pray for us.

THE DEATH OF ST. CLARE OF ASSISI

By Theresa Zoe Williams

St. Clare (1194–1253) had long suffered illness, and the day after the Holy Father delivered to her the papal approval which officially recognized her order, she prepared to welcome a happy death. All of the little sisters kept vigil around her, weeping and fasting and praying.

From her deathbed in the morning, Clare looked out through a large window that overlooked the countryside from Assisi and took in the glorious morning light. But it was not just an ordinary natural light that came through the window—Clare and all of the sisters present turned in the direction of this great light, enraptured.

There then, from the countryside, floated into St. Clare's little room a procession of virgins clothed all in white, each wearing a golden crown, and from their midst came forth the great Virgin of virgins—the Blessed Virgin Mary. And on her head, the Blessed Virgin wore a crown of such resplendent beauty that it completely outshined the sun.

Then, Mary came forward towards Clare's bed. She stood over the dying saint and sweetly embraced her and, while doing so, motioned for the other virgins to bring her a tunic of pure gold, laden with precious stones. The Blessed Mother then clothed her very soul with this magnificent garb, and Clare was taken by this retinue of virgins to paradise, leaving only her lifeless corpse behind on her bed linens.

The story appears to be fiction, incredible, and unearthly. But that was the sort of devotion Clare lived and pressed on her followers: incredible and unearthly

St. Clare of Assisi, pray for us.

ST. BENEDICT'S DRAGON

By Brooke Gregory

Most have heard of St. Benedict (d. 547). The saint whose medal (which you might be wearing right now) protects against poisoning and the devil, the saint who founded cenobitic monastic life that removed monks from the world when stuff in the fast-crumbling Western arm of the Roman Empire was starting to get real.

His Rule is known for bringing a quiet rhythm to the lives of those who follow it, and the abbeys that bear his name are famous for being places of retreat and silence. There is even an awesome liquor associated with the Order called Benedictine. The overall image we have of him is pretty chill: a quiet, wise, bearded old man who hated sin and the devil.

What we rarely hear about is that beneath all the beard and the prayer vigils lay a desert-dwelling Jedi Master who literally beat the daylights out of demons and had no problem telling terrifying Goth warlords where they could shove it. St. Benedict was a lean, mean, ascetic machine, and the

devil himself knew better than to mess with him. He super-
naturally warded off assassination attempts and worked miracles like it was just "business as usual." But one particular
miracle he worked tops them all. It's difficult to even classify
it as a miracle. More properly, it was a supernatural prank,
and if the internet were a thing back then, this one would
have gone viral.

In one of his monasteries, St. Benedict counseled a monk
who was prone to inconstancy in his vocation and couldn't
make up his mind whether he wanted to leave the cloister or
stay. Finally, Benedict got so fed up with the young upstart
that he told him to leave. St. Gregory relates in his *Life of
St. Benedict* that the monk had barely cleared the monastery
gates when he met an enormous dragon that lunged at him,
gaping his terrifying jaws wide open to swallow him whole.

Understandably freaked out beyond all recognition, he
screamed for the brothers to come help him because *Oh
my gosh! Random dragon!* The brothers came running out
because seeing a prodigal monk get eaten by a dragon is the
closest they probably ever got to quality entertainment out
there in the wilderness.

They were sadly disappointed, though, because all they
saw was a young monk running about waving his arms and
screaming about a fire-breathing lizard-beast that was most
certainly not there.

The poor boy ran straight back into the monastery where
he promised Benedict to never leave ever again. It was then
revealed that Benedict had conjured the phantom dragon
through prayer in order to keep the monk true to his
vocation.

And you thought your spiritual director was harsh. All things in love and devotion.

St. Benedict, pray for us.

ST. MARGARET'S DRAGON

By Brooke Gregory

St. Margaret of Antioch (289–304), also known as Marina by the Eastern Churches, is one of the Fourteen Holy Helpers and was one of the saints whose voice was heard by Joan of Arc. She is a martyr of the early Church, and her cult was wildly popular in the Medieval era when it spread from the East all across Europe. Stories about her are varied and uncertain, but most traditions place her in Antioch during the reign of the notorious Roman emperor Diocletian.

Her father was a pagan priest who cast her out of his home in shame after her conversion, forcing her to take up life as a shepherdess. She was also "pretty," and after she refused the advances of a high-ranking Roman official, she was outed as a Christian to the local government, and after several tortures and execution attempts, she gave up her life for the Faith.

Of all her experiences during her martyrdom, one of the craziest stories that keeps being told is the episode for which she became venerated as the patron of childbirth—in a roundabout sort of way. Even the author of *The Golden Legend*, a thirteenth-century collection of hagiographies in which her story is preserved, found that it pushed the bounds of believability.

It is told that Margaret, after having endured innumerable tortures at the hands of the local government, was confronted by Satan in the form of a monstrous dragon. The dragon promptly ate her; it literally ate her.

Tradition varies as to what happened next: most simply state that because of her holiness, the dragon could not keep her down and—to use the polite term most traditions feature—"disgorged" her.

Others prefer the more dramatic version in which, before taking a trip down the dragon's gullet, Margaret managed to grab a cross nearby and hold on to it. Not one to wait for the dragon to lose his lunch, she took that cross in her hand and *punched straight through the dragon's stomach with it*, clawing her way out.

St. Margaret of Antioch, pray for us.

CAN THESE STORIES BE ALLEGORICAL?

By Shaun McAfee

Yes, absolutely, some saint stories *can* be read with some allegorical nuances.

Plenty of saints have the credit of punching, throwing, or otherwise duking it out with demons to their name, but St. Margaret alone has the distinction of literally ripping Satan apart.

The astonishing saint story is told as history by every source, but interpretations have often compared this event as an allegory for the re-birthing of her faith: she escaped from the dragon (of paganism) as if being born. For this reason, she has long been considered an intercessor for women in childbirth, which is all at once comforting and terrifying, all things considered.

Readers can apply the lens of allegory to some stories like this, but it comes with a price. And that price is a type of reductionism, where we cut the Faith down to man's level where nothing spontaneous, nothing absurd, nothing terrifying, nothing glorious happens. Excepting the astonishing things the saints did and experiences as farfetched really deals a blow to the Faith itself—the power of the Gospel. Not to mention, it diminishes the reality of the supernatural works of angels and the uncanny works of the devil. If we're not willing to believe that St. Benedict literally fought demon dragons, we've reduced the saint, and by virtue of that, we've reduced our own faith.

That's not to say there are not stories within stories—but you can have it *both* ways! You are free to believe that St. Margaret was swallowed by a dragon (Jonah was swallowed by a whale!), and you can also believe that that dragon and her holy slaughter was a direct representation of the fight of every Christian. St. Paul preached this exact message when he explained to the Ephesians, "For we are not contending against flesh and blood, but against the principalities, against the powers, against the world rulers of this present darkness, against the spiritual hosts of wickedness in the heavenly places" (6:12).

FIREPROOF: ST. IRENE OF CHRYSOVALANTOU

By Brooke Gregory

When it came to the spiritual life, Irene of Chryso-valantou was a woman who did not play around. Erstwhile fiancée of the heir to the Byzantine Empire in the ninth century, Irene gave up her comfortable life as a young noble and entered a monastery in Constantinople. There she quickly gained a reputation for sanctity, standing all day and all night in prayer.

After only a few years at the monastery, she was offered the office of abbess after the previous abbess fell asleep in the Lord. Although reluctant, she accepted.

To help her, her guardian angel stood constantly at her side, forewarning her of events pertinent to the monastery and the souls under her care. She battled with evil magicians, ordered demons to leave the possessed, and when she prayed in the monastery courtyard at night, she would levitate while the cypresses before her bowed to her until she blessed them. She was even given apples from heaven by St. John the Apostle himself, which possessed supernatural abilities to sustain the physical and spiritual strength of anyone who ate the smallest slice.

As meek and gentle as she seemed to her sisters in the monastery and the faithful who visited her for counsel, a fascinating miracle attributed to her is testimony to the steel backbone she possessed.

One night as she stood at prayer, Irene was assaulted by demons in a terrifyingly physical manner. They screamed at her, they blasphemed God, and asked her how long she would continue burning them with her prayers. When she remained unfazed, they lit candles from her votive lamp and struck up an undeniably creepy sing-song taunt: "Wooden Irene, wooden feet hold you up! How long will you burn us?"

While they sang, they set her veil on fire. Irene remained unmoved. She prayed as the fire spread, burning through her habit into the flesh of her shoulders and back. One of the sisters smelled the smoke from her cell and came running into the sanctuary. She immediately began beating out the fire while Irene was suspended in prayer as though nothing were happening.

When the fire was out, she actually scolded the nun saying, "My child, you thought you were doing a praiseworthy act, but you could not see that an angel stood before me weaving a wreath of marvelous flowers! He stretched forth to place it on my head, but when you put out the fire, he disappeared."

As she was speaking, an overpowering fragrance of flowers filled the entire monastery and lingered for days while the nuns glorified God for the miracle. It is now a custom in some places for priests to bless flowers in her name, which the faithful burn in their homes in times of sickness or distress.

St. Irene of Chrysovalantou, pray for us.

THE WILD, BILOCATING DEATH OF ST. MARY OF EGYPT

By Brooke Gregory

The Desert Fathers get a lot well-deserved credit. They blazed the trail for monasticism as we know it today and thrived in conditions that threatened to break their bodies and their spirits. But among them were also the Desert Mothers: women who fled the world either alone or in community and were sought-out by laypeople for their spiritual wisdom gained from heroic ascetic struggles.

Unique among them is St. Mary of Egypt (344–421), a penitent and Desert Mother who would have gone unheralded had she not crossed paths with a desert-dwelling monk named Zosimas. When they met, Mary displayed a stunning gift of clairvoyance, calling Zosimas by name although they had never met. She was known by those who observed her to have walked on water, levitated during prayer, and she had an extensive knowledge of Scripture despite having never studied it and hardly ever entering a church in her life. By her own admission, she experienced terrible demonic assaults from which she was delivered by apparitions of the Mother of God.

A most epic part of Mary's life was her miraculous manner of death. When they first met, Mary had dwelt in the desert completely and utterly alone for years. After she revealed her former sinful life and conversion to Zosimas, she begged him to meet her at sunset on the banks of the Jordan to give her Holy Communion. He did so, and afterward she told him to meet her at the exact spot where they first met in the middle of the desert, one exact year from that day.

He agreed and went back to his monastery rejoicing but told no one of what he had seen. St. Mary of Egypt had sworn him to silence until after they met again a year later. The year passed, and Zosimas set out to fulfill his promise.

When he reached the spot of their first meeting, he found her body neatly laid out on the ground—it appeared as if she were only sleeping. Next to her was a message written in the desert sand that expressed her desire for a proper burial and revealed that she had died the same day and hour she had received the Holy Mysteries a year earlier—miles and miles away from the spot where she now lay.

Stunned and realizing in amazement that she had been miraculously transported from the banks of the Jordan, Zosimas began to dig her grave while chanting Psalms and prayers. He found the digging hard going and was terrified when he looked up and suddenly found a fearsome lion at his side digging up the hard-packed earth with its strong paws. When he realized the creature was sent by God to assist him, he shrugged, *"okay,"* and buried Mary of Egypt beneath the desert that had been her salvation.

He returned to his monastery and told the brothers there of the miraculous and holy Desert Mother he had met. Her epic story was passed down from generation to generation of monks until it was finally preserved in writing by St. Sophronius, patriarch of Jerusalem, and remains a blessing to those seeking deliverance from sins of the flesh and demonic attacks.

God delivers those who trust in him.

St. Mary of Egypt, pray for us.

BEST MIRACLE EVER: BRIGID OF KILDARE

By Brooke Gregory

St. Brigid of Kildare (d. 523) is one of those saints who enjoys universal veneration in both Western and Eastern Rites of the Church. Known as "Mary of the Gaels" in her native Ireland, the list of miracles attributed to her during her earthly life alone could fill a book. Many of them have to do with multiplying or miraculously providing some form of physical nourishment—butter, milk, and her specialty: beer. A famous prayer attributed to her expresses her desire for "a great lake of beer for the King of Kings" which all the hosts of heaven could enjoy for eternity.

She was a woman of great generosity and hospitality, and she showed the love of God to those around her by miraculously supplying them with all the good things of creation. Of all her miracles, two stand out for being particularly noteworthy in the beer department (or aisle?). In one instance, she is said to have supplied eighteen churches in her district with beer from a single barrel to last from Maundy Thursday through the end of Eastertide, mirroring her Lord's miracle of multiplying bread and fish to feed his hungry followers. She certainly knew how to spread the joy of Christ's resurrection!

Another time, she was serving a community of lepers that found itself woefully deprived of beer, which was a precious commodity in those days when water was easily contaminated but not easily procured. The people there begged her for more and she obliged. Again mirroring a miracle of her Lord, she transformed the water used for baths into beer—not just any beer, but as most sources specify, "excellent beer." Best miracle ever!

When Brigid did something, she did it right. She also performed this particular miracle regularly for visiting clerics. Hospitality was an extremely important virtue among the ancient Celts, and beer was its physical manifestation. Taking "waste not, want not" to miraculous extremes, Brigid would transform her dirty bathwater into the finest beer to serve to her guests, and it's never stated that anyone was the wiser, which is probably for the best. Maybe she should be the patron saint of recycling too.

St. Brigid of Kildare, pray for us.

BE CAREFUL WHO YOU PUNISH: ST. MARINA "THE MONK"

By Brooke Gregory

We often like to think of the saints as well-behaved people who follow the rules and live serene lives. Nothing could be further from the truth.

While many of the saints did have uneventful and solitary lives, many had to go to great lengths to serve the Lord. Some exhibited behavior that most of us—including other generations and cultures—would consider weird or socially unacceptable at best. One of these saints was Marina the Monk (fifth or eighth century). Yes, Marina the *Monk*.

A saint from the Maronite tradition, Marina had designs to become a nun. Her father had other plans. He desired to sell her into marriage to the first suitable candidate and retire to a monastery. When he told her that he had no idea what to do with her, that she was a useless woman, Marina was having none of that.

The next day, she left and entered the nearest monastery as a monk named Marinus with her father, and no one was the wiser for decades. Marina's life in the monastery was outwardly uneventful, but one act of humility from her changed several people's lives forever.

One day after Marina's father had passed away, the abbot sent Marina with two other monks into the nearest town to do business for the monastery. They stayed at an inn where a Roman solider was also lodging. The soldier and innkeeper's daughter had a secret liaison during his visit and he threatened the girl not to tell, convincing her to place the blame on "Marinus the monk" if she fell pregnant.

The innkeeper's daughter discovered she was pregnant a few weeks later and pointed the finger at Marina, who made no attempt to deny the accusation, even flinging herself down in tears before the abbot and confessing. Furious, the abbot sent her away from the monastery where she lived outside the gates as a beggar.

The innkeeper's daughter abandoned her baby with Marina, who cared for it as her own child for ten years without complaint, surviving on alms. Eventually, the monks convinced the abbot to let "Marinus" back in. Marina was admitted but under severe penalty: she was given the worst and most disgusting menial tasks in the monastery. She did these duties in silence and humility until her death of illness at age forty.

So, did they ever find out?

When her body was cleaned and prepared for burial, her

true identity was discovered, to the astonishment—and probably the embarrassment—of the entire monastery. The abbot wept bitterly beside her deathbed for how harshly he had treated her and informed the innkeeper, who sought repentance. God sent spiritual torments to both the Roman solider and innkeeper's daughter to bring them to repentance, and they confessed their sins before Marina's grave. Several healings were reported during Marina's funeral services at the monastery.

Guard your eyes, but don't completely shut them to the good deeds of others.

St. Marina "the Monk," pray for us.

ST. LAWRENCE, THE HOLY GRAIL, AND THE TREASURES OF ROME

By Deacon Marty McIndoe

The extraordinary (and riotous) story of the martyrdom of Lawrence (225–258) is known to many (and is told in this book), but few know the additional stories surrounding the Holy Grail—yes, *that one*. Many imagine, due to popular recent fiction, that the chalice is lost to history, but thanks to Lawrence, it is not.

Story tradition holds that the chalice that was used in the Last Supper of our Lord, sometimes known as the "Holy Grail," was brought out of Israel to Rome by St. Peter. All of the succeeding popes used that chalice. Even in the canon of the liturgy of the time, which has been preserved, is a reference to the vessel as "this most famous chalice" during the Eucharistic prayers.

St. Lawrence understood the incredible value of this most precious artifact, and knew that it had to be saved. So he gave it to Precilio, a trusted Roman Christian soldier from Hispania (modern-day Spain). Lawrence asked Precilio to bring the chalice to Huesca in Aragon. He chose Huesca for a simple reason: it was where Lawrence's parents were living.

Precilio brought it there for safe keeping. In the early 700s, the Muslims began invading Hispania. The chalice was moved to the monastery of San Juan de la Pena in the Pyrenees to keep it safe from the ensuing Muslims. It remained hidden there until 1399 when King Martin of Aragon reclaimed it and brought it to Zaragoza.

When Valencia became capital of Aragon in the fifteenth century, King Alfonso V of Aragon moved it to Valencia. It has been in the Cathedral of Valencia ever since.

Two modern popes have used the Chalice: John Paul II in 1982 and Pope Benedict XVI in 2006. When Pope Benedict used it for Mass, he used the words "this most famous chalice" as used in the Eucharistic liturgy by all of the early popes. We have the foresight of St. Lawrence to thank for ensuring that Rome, sacked over and over, would not give up the precious artifact.

St. Lawrence, pray for us.

BEHIND ENEMY LINES: ST. FRANCIS OF ASSISI

By Deacon Marty McIndoe

F rancesco Bernardone (1181–1226) sought the face of Christ in every aspect of living after his personal conversion to Christ. In his attempts to totally live out the Gospel message, to most of us and even some of his followers, the future St. Francis of Assisi went to extremes.

A striking example of this was in Jesus's teaching for love of our enemies. This emanated in Francis's meeting with the sultan, Malek al Kamil, who was the nephew of Saladin and leader of the Muslim forces fighting the Christians, in 1219. This was the time of the Fifth Crusade and there was great consternation between the Western civilization and the Muslims. Western Christendom had been at war with the Eastern Muslims for over 120 years at this point, and Francis wanted to do whatever he could to stop the bloodshed.

He decided, through prayer, that he needed to meet with

the sultan of Egypt. Some of his contemporaries thought that Francis knew that this could mean certain death and that he wanted to do it anyway so that he could die a martyr. Others believed that it was just his love for all peoples and hatred of war that enticed him to go. Nonetheless, Francis and his companion, Illuminato, left to go visit the sultan in Egypt.

Francis and Brother Illuminato reached the battlefield between the Christians and the Muslims right after a very fierce and bloody clash. Both sides had declared a temporary truce to recover from their last battle. Still, it was quite dangerous to try to cross over to the Muslim side.

On their way to the Muslim territory, Francis and Illuminato came across two lambs. Francis was overjoyed to see the lambs and said to Illuminato, "Trust in the Lord, brother, for the Gospel is being fulfilled in us: Behold, I am sending you forth like sheep in the midst of wolves."

Shortly after saying this, the wolves descended upon them as Saracen sentries. What made the entire event convenient (and providential) is that the Saracens brought Francis and Illuminato directly to the sultan, just where Francis wanted to be.

When they were brought before the sultan, he asked Francis who had sent him there. Francis told the sultan that it was Almighty God who had sent him to proclaim to the sultan, and his people, the way of salvation and to proclaim the Gospel. Francis put a challenge to sultan saying that he should build a large fire and have the Muslim priests enter it along with Francis and that God would show that only Francis would survive and that the true and holy faith would then be known. The sultan told Francis that he could not accept this challenge because he feared a revolt among his people. The sultan seemed to like Francis and tried to shower him with many gifts, but because of his love of poverty, Francis did not accept the gifts, causing the sultan to further respect Francis.

After remaining in camp several days, the sultan had given the duo permission to safely visit the Holy Lands if they wished. When it came time for Francis to leave, the sultan petitioned him, "Pray for me that God may reveal to me the law and the faith that is more pleasing to him." It is interesting that Crusader and Franciscan journals alike mention this visit, but no Islamic mention is made. There is a legend that the sultan had a death bed conversion to Christianity, but we can't know for sure.

The fruits of this visit can still be seen today in the Holy Lands. Because of the respectful relationship between the sultan and Francis, only the Franciscans were given permission to maintain religious sites within the Holy Lands. This was a gift given by the Muslims even after the Christians had suffered defeat in the Crusades. When you visit the Holy Lands, the Franciscan presence at most of the holy sites is widely seen. They have been there since 1229, thanks to Francis and the sultan.

A simple charity and peace can last centuries.

St. Francis and companion Illuminato, pray for us.

ST. SEBASTIAN: TWICE MURDERED

By Deacon Marty McIndoe

Sebastian (d. 288) was the son of wealthy Roman parents and was educated in Milan. Although exact historical accounts differ and it is difficult to separate history from legend, most sources indicate that he was an officer in the Roman army who worked as the captain of the guard.

A convert, he initially hid his Christian beliefs from the Romans so that he could minister to the many Christians who were either isolated in their prisons or who were being mistreated or abused by the Romans.

During Diocletian's persecution of the Christians, Sebastian visited the Christians in prison, bringing them food and comfort. Two Christians in the prison were about to face their death and were so discouraged that they were about to give up their faith. Sebastian made such an impassioned exhortation to them that they gained strength and stood firm in their beliefs. It is told that his appeal was so great that he converted the other prisoners who had heard him.

There are accounts of Sebastian converting many other people as well. One account tells us that Sebastian cured the very sick wife of another Roman army officer simply by drawing the Sign of the Cross on her forehead. This small act was enough to convert the soldier's wife, the soldier, and his whole family.

Another account recounts that when he finally did come forward to his local prefect about his being a Christian, he was so convincing that the prefect and his son converted to the Faith. That son later became a saint too.

Another story tells us that Sebastian converted a local governor and his wife to Christianity. The governor's wife had been unable to speak until her conversion, and then regained her speech. This same governor, after his conversion to Christianity, set free all the Christians who were in prison, and he then resigned his position as governor. A new governor was sent in, and this new governor was so upset at all that Sebastian had done, he had Sebastian arrested for being a Christian and sentenced to death; Sebastian was to be tied to a tree and killed by a squad of archers.

The martyrdom tells that the Mauritanian archers shot him over and over with arrows. They left him tied to the tree presuming he had died. But when one of his disciples (who became St. Irene) went to get his body for burial, she found that he was still alive.

She nursed him back to health and begged him to escape from that territory. Sebastian refused to leave. Instead, Sebastian went to Emperor Diocletian and condemned him for his treatment of the Christians. Diocletian, among the most infamous of Roman persecutors, was furious and ordered Sebastian to death, this time by beating and clubbing him. The sentence was carried out the next day. After the guards were sure that Sebastian was dead from the severe beating, they dumped his bloody corpse into the Roman sewer system.

One of Sebastian's disciples, a widow, received a dream telling her to go to a nearby field to find the body of Sebastian. His body was found: it was completely free of any bruises or signs of beating. He was buried on the Appian Way near to the catacombs that bear his name. A basilica, which is one of the seven chief churches of Rome, was built over his grave in 367, less than a century later.

Since Sebastian had been ordered to death twice, he is known as the saint who was murdered twice and was an inspiration to millions during the Black Plague.

St. Sebastian, pray for us.

SIMEON STYLITES: WORLD RECORD HOLDER

By Deacon Marty McIndoe

Simeon (388–459) is a fifth century ascetic saint who, to this day, holds a record in the Guinness Book of World Records. The record is for sitting on a pillar for forty-seven years. It was quite a challenge, considering the temperatures in the modern Syrian Desert have ranged from over one hundred degrees to the tens below zero. Simeon sat on a small platform on the very top of a pillar, no matter the conditions.

He was born in what is modern day Turkey in the year 388. He was the son of a shepherd and his family was Christian. One day, when he was thirteen years old, he heard a sermon on the beatitudes that moved him so much that he wanted to deepen his Christian faith through sacrifice and contemplation. Three years later, he joined a monastery and practiced such severe sacrifice and penance that the monastery asked him to leave!

After leaving the monastery, Simeon fasted from food and water for the full forty days of Lent. As reports of his self-denial spread, people would come to him asking for prayers and just to be near this holy man. In order to avoid these crowds of people, he fled to a mountaintop cave in Syria.

When admirers followed him even to there, he decided to try to escape them vertically rather than horizontally. He found a nine-foot pillar that had a square platform on top and moved there. In good charity, local youth boys would occasionally climb the pillar to bring him scraps of food and goat milk.

Since the crowds kept coming to him, even on top of the pillar, he built the pillar higher so that his platform was now some fifty feet above the ground. That didn't stop the people from coming, and so, once a day, he would deliver a sermon from the top of the pillar. Many people, including local rulers and Emperors Theodosius II and Leo I, sought him out for his holiness, prayers, and words of wisdom. He wrote letters from the pillar—many of which are still extant today—and was seen as a real gift from God to the people around him.

When Simeon became very sick, the emperor, Theodosius II, sent three bishops to Simeon begging him to come down for medical assistance. He refused to leave his platform and eventually became well again. Simeon refused to see even his own mother, saying that hopefully they would meet again in the kingdom of heaven. He would not come down for any cause, and when his mother died, the people brought the mother's coffin to the pillar for the funeral service because he further refused to leave the pillar.

A disciple found him dead in the year 459 in the position of prayer. The patriarch of Antioch, Martyrius, celebrated this monk's funeral in front of a huge crowd of people. They buried him near his pillar. Years later, the saint was honored with a large Byzantine church, enclosing about 53,000 square feet. Four basilicas, oriented in the cardinal directions, formed a cross and surrounded an octagonal court encompassing Simeon's famous pillar. The ruins of the Church of St. Simeon the Stylite, with only the base of his famous pillar surviving, are a UNESCO World Heritage site in Syria.

Stylos in Greek means "pillar." To this day, no one has come close to challenging his Guinness World Record. Ain't nobody gonna break his style.

St. Simeon Stylites, pray for us.

POPE ST. CLEMENT I: WATER DIVINER

By Deacon Marty McIndoe

Clement (AD 35–99) was a disciple of both St. Peter and St. Paul and became the fourth bishop of Rome (88–99). He is also considered the first Apostolic Father of the Early Church. Clement was known as one who sat at the feet of the apostles and listened to their words about Jesus. In the year 96, he wrote an epistle to the Church in Corinth in which he asserts and confirms the apostolic authority of the bishops and presbyters (priests) as rulers of the visible hierarchy of the Church on earth. He also wrote the deacons were in a position of service to these bishops and priests.

During the reign of Emperor Trajan, when Mamertinus was prefect of the city, some of the citizens of Rome rebelled against the Christians, and especially against Clement. Mamertinus wanted to avoid a riot and had Clement arrested and sent to the emperor, who ordered his

banishment to Pontus (today this is the Black Sea), where
he was condemned to work in the marble quarries there. In
these work quarries, he found many fellow Christians who
had also been banished there to perform hard labor. The
work was extremely harsh and the only source of water for
the laborers was about six miles away.

Clement knew that he had to find a closer place for water,
but none could be found—not naturally. One day, while
working, he saw a lamb on the side of a hill scratching at the
ground with its hoof. Clement took this as a sign and went
to the spot and began digging there. Shortly after, he found
a spring that gushed water up. The workers were, of course,
amazed beyond belief and believed that it was a gift from
God. Many of the convicts who were not Christians were so
moved by this miracle that they converted to Christianity.

The quarry officials were upset about this mass conversion
and they brought Clement to Aufidianus, the local prefect,
who ordered the execution of Clement. He told the soldiers
to take him to the Black Sea, put an anchor around his neck,
and throw him into the waters, which they did.

Clements's disciple Phoebus went with some of the other
disciples of Clement to try to retrieve his body. Tradition
tells us that when they went to the Black Sea, the sea withdrew three miles to expose Clement's remains and that those
remains were already encased in a beautiful shrine. They left
the shrine and all of his remains right where they were found.

Another tradition tells us that every year after that, on the
same day, the sea would withdraw and reveal the shrine. A
story has been passed to us that one year, a young boy went
out to visit the shrine and never came back. Locals assumed

the boy was caught in the rising tide and had drowned. The next year, when the waters again withdrew and exposed the shrine, they found the boy alive and sleeping in the shrine and brought him home.

Tall tale? Well, in the year 860, St. Cyril recovered the bones from the shrine and brought them to Constantinople. Some of the relics were left there and then some were brought back to Rome and put into the Church of San Clemente, where they are still reverently preserved. Consistent with the story, in sacred art, St. Clement is usually depicted with an anchor indicating his martyrdom, and many of the oldest paintings and frescos depict his famous shrine on the sea floor.

St. Clement I, pray for us.

ST. DENIS OF PARI: THE SAINT WHO LOST HIS HEAD BUT KEPT ON GOING

By Deacon Marty McIndoe

Around the year 250, Pope Fabian sent several missionaries to the Gaul region, today's France. The most popular of these—even at the time—was Denis, who would become popularly regarded as the patron saint of France.

Denis was known for his holiness and trustworthiness to follow through with any task and was a sure choice for the pope's interests in planting churches in Gaul. Denis settled on an island in the middle of the Seine River in Lutetia, which is now known as Paris.

He and his companions, the priest Rusticus and the deacon Eleutherius, built a church on that island and began ministering to and converting the people of that area. Denis quickly became known for his fearless and indefatigable preaching—no matter the conditions, Denis preached. Through his efforts, many people converted and returned to the Christian faith.

But local pagan priests became so angered at this that they went to the Roman authorities asking for these Christians to be dealt with—seeking their execution. With the anti-Christian backing of Emperor Decius, the authorities were quite willing to carry out a sentence.

It is reported that numerous attempts to kill members of this fraternal community were made but were unsuccessful. Eventually, the Roman authorities captured Denis and had him beheaded in a public audience at what is today Montmartre (Mount of the Martyr).

Remember, no matter the conditions, Denis preached. So, after having his head removed, he picked up his own head with his two hands and proceeded to finish his sermon in the streets of Lutetia. He walked over two miles with his head in his hands—a story numerous Lutetians and future Parisians corroborated as eyewitnesses to be preserved. Tradition says he even paused for a moment to wash the blood from his face in order to preach more clearly. When he finally found a suitable spot, he lay down, with his head in his hands, and died. He is buried there and the Basilica of St. Denis marks this spot.

Around the world and frequently in Paris today, pilgrims will find many statues of a bishop holding his own head. Travelers will see this at Notre Dame Cathedral, on the island where St. Denis first built his church. One may also notice his statues in many parks and city areas. There is a street originally named St. Denis Street and there is a very large abbey church built in the town of St. Denis about four miles north of Paris. This abbey is the Basilica of St. Denis and is built over the place where St. Denis, St. Rusticus, and St. Eleutherius were buried. Over the ages, this has become a significant holy place and a place of national interest. St. Joan of Arc hung her battle arms there in 1429.

An indefatigable preacher for sure! A finer observation might be that because he was preaching, it must be assumed that people were listening. But how infinitely difficult it must have been to evade listening to a man preaching with only a neck at the top and holding his head in his hands! The Church, in all of its subtlety—and perhaps comicality—tells us that Denis is the saint to pray for intercessions when suffering from severe headaches.

St. Denis, pray for us.

ARE WE REALLY EXPECTED TO BELIEVE THESE STORIES?

By Shaun McAfee

It is tempting to fictionalize a story like that of St. Denis or St. Mary of Egypt. The early saint stories are filled with unlikely and unimaginable outcomes. But even when we look at recent saints like Francis of Assisi or Francis Xavier, we see some pretty tremendous situations and miracles through their faith and works. And modern saints like Padre Pio and John Vianney also had a host of utterly absurd events and miracles attributed to them. These were performed at a time when the Church was subject to scientific investigations and claims of the miraculous were no exception.

It's tempting to call these stories into question. Surely, we should feel almost normal to consider the credibility of saints fighting dragons and others surviving being burned alive. It's okay to be speculative, but speculative only to a certain measure. The Bible is full of startling miracles that defy all logic and physical science. The Bible tells stories like Elijah's bones bringing a man back to life, Daniel surviving a night in a den full of lions, Paul handling a viper as if it were nothing, and Peter raising people from the dead!

If we can accept these miracles as true, we have little reason not to expect the stories of the saints to be absolutely true. We should remind ourselves of the words of Christ from the Gospel of Mark.

"'Which is easier, to say to the paralytic, "Your sins are forgiven," or to say, "Rise, take up your pallet and walk"? But that you may know that the Son of man has authority on earth to forgive sins'—he said to the paralytic—'I say to you, rise, take up your pallet and go home.' And he rose, and immediately took up the pallet and went out before them all; so that they were all amazed and glorified God, saying, 'We never saw anything like this!'" (Mk 2:9–12).

If we are to deny miracles, then we are to reject the numerous incalculable miracles performed by Jesus. Putting an ear back on, changing water into wine, and so on. Not just the miracles of Jesus, but also the miracles and wonders of those who follow him: the saints!

If Christians accept the truth of the Bible, they should expect even more from the saints. This is true, since Jesus said, "Truly, truly, I say to you, he who believes in me will also do the works that I do; and greater works than these will he do because I go to the Father" (Jn 14:12). We are, assuredly, called to better things.

Miracles do occur, especially when the saints are involved.

LIGHT AND EASY: ST. JOSEPH OF CUPERTINO

By Deacon Marty McIndoe

Is levitation real? Well, it is mentioned frequently in the lives of the saints. Some saints associated with levitation are Saints Margaret of Hungary, Stephen of Hungary, Mary of Egypt, Francis of Paola, and Martin de Porres, among many others. However, you could say the Maverick of levitation is Joseph of Cupertino (1603–1663). We have over seventy documented times where he levitated, often for extended periods of time.

Joseph was born in a stable, just like Jesus. His father had been a poor carpenter who died just before Joseph's birth. His mother was quite poor too and had lost her home. Though they had no money, Joseph's mother was a very devout woman and taught Joseph about the love of God.

He began having mystical visions as a young child. He often seemed aloof to the other children because he focused so much on higher ideas, and they called him "open mouth" because of his gaping manner. Aside from his mystical nature, he acquired a very bad temper and found formal learning too difficult, failed to read well, and was thought to be quite dumb.

What they didn't know was that his gaping nature and aloofness was due to ecstatic moments of prayer—even as a youth. Besides being incredibly lacking in cleverness, he had a hard time holding onto a job. Because almost nobody else would keep him, Joseph was able to find a job caring for the horses at a Franciscan convent near Cupertino. The Franciscans there quickly noted his holiness, humility, and obedience and began grooming him to become a Franciscan. Joseph began studying for the priesthood, but being a poor student made it difficult. Fortunately, some of the friars helped him and he was ordained a deacon and eventually a priest. Even though Joseph was a poor student, he had a divine knowledge that allowed him to solve many difficult theological problems.

Joseph found it difficult to be a priest because he would so often levitate and enter into ecstasy—he really could not concentrate because he was so rapt when he prayed. This happened at nearly every Mass he celebrated, and because of this, the Franciscan Order finally had to ban him from saying Mass in public. For the next thirty-five years, he was often moved from one friary to another due to being so disruptive.

On one Christmas Eve, he invited real life shepherds to join in celebrating the birth of Jesus. When they began playing their bagpipes and flutes, he let out a screaming cry of joy and flew straight through the air to the altar. The congregation watched, astonished, as he remained suspended above the altar for at least fifteen minutes. One onlooker noted that when he levitated and flew, his garments remained completely still, like a statue.

Another time a priest remarked to Joseph how beautifully God had created the heavens. Joseph immediately flew up and rested on the top of an olive tree. The observers said that the tree branch barely moved, almost as if a small sparrow had perched on it—light as the Holy Spirit.

Unfortunately, a jealous and skeptical priest brought Joseph before the Inquisition. They asked Joseph to say Mass in their presence. He did just as they had requested and immediately launched to the main altar and remained above the altar saying the Mass. The nuns were unraveled in anger because they thought his robes would catch on fire from the candles. Yet they didn't and he returned to the floor unharmed. The Inquisition let him go on his way and never entertained another complaint about the future saint.

But his ecstasies still had sceptics of every kind and origin. Probably the most prominent witness to Joseph's levitation and flying is Pope Urban VIII. Joseph went to Rome with his father general and had an audience with the pope.

The moment Joseph bent down in front of the pontiff, he immediately began to levitate. He came down as soon as the father general ordered him. Urban VIII told the father general that he marveled at what had just happened and would be happy to testify at a future canonization process if he ever had the opportunity.

Altogether, there are over seventy recorded, verified

statements concerning the levitation of Joseph of Cupertino. Sometimes his levitation would last six or seven hours! Joseph died in 1663.

Even if you aren't given the outward gifts of levitation, the burden laid upon you by your Master, Christ Jesus, is light, sweet, and easy; consoling to any soul's state of heaviness.

St. Joseph of Cupertino, pray for us.

ST. QUITERIA THE "NONUPLET" AND HER SISTER GANG OF WARRIORS

By Deacon Marty McIndoe

Quiteria (d. second century) was born in the early centuries of the Church in Minho, Portugal. Her father was a high-ranking Roman military officer and she was the lastborn of nine girls. They were all born on the same day of the year. Her sisters were Eumelia, Liberata, Gema, Genebra, Germana, Basilissa, Marina, and Vitoria. Try running through that list when your kid is misbehaving!

Quiteria's mother was so upset that she had given birth to nine girls, like a common animal in her opinion, that she told her maid named Sila, a good Christian, to take all of the babies and throw them into the river. The maid could not complete the mother's orders, so she brought all nine of the children—some much older by then—to a Christian monk in a remote town where they grew up together in a Christian community. The father, usually away in the summer on Roman war marches, was unaware of their birth until the mother told him what she had ordered.

The sisters grew strong in their Christian beliefs and in their commitment to each other. They formed together a nine-sister warrior gang that went about the country toppling Roman deity statues and breaking Christians out of Roman jails. They even went so far as to wage a small guerrilla war against the Romans. This led them back to their father, Lucio, who recognized the girls as his daughters and found out what his wife had done. He then tried to take them back into his home and tried to turn them from Christianity to the Roman gods. When they refused, he had them all jailed.

It is said that while they were in jail, they gave thanks, praised God, and preached the Gospel from their chains so well that they converted other prisoners. After many months behind bars, an angel appeared to them and broke them out of jail and they continued to irritate the Romans.

The girls were arrested a second time and again imprisoned. Again, they converted many of their fellow inmates and this time also the guards, and once more, an angel set them free. They went back to their guerilla war tactics against the Romans, repeating the whole cycle without fear or hesitation.

Their bravery led some of the girls to their deaths, but we are told that Quiteria and Marina and Liberata were captured again, and after a short time in jail, they were beheaded. These three have been canonized.

It is also said that their sister Euphemia escaped from the soldiers who pursued her and threw herself from a cliff situated today in the Peneda-Gerês National Park (it is called today *Penedo da Santa*, Cliff of the Saint). Tradition of their story tells that a rock opened up and swallowed her, and on that spot, a hot spring opened up from the earth.

After Quiteria was beheaded, they threw her into the sea. But that was not the end for Quiteria. Her cult reported in early stories that she was seen coming out of the sea, carrying her head, and walked to the Church of the Virgin Mary. It is interesting to note that St. Quiteria is known for her patronage against rabies. This is because she had held two rabid dogs at bay, just with her voice.

Family ties can be thicker than blood, but the Faith is always stronger than death.

St. Quiteria, pray for us.

POPE ST. JOHN PAUL II: HEALER

By Deacon Marty McIndoe

This story begins in Costa Rica. Pope John Paul II (1978–2005) loved the Americas, and he certainly loved the poor in South and Central America. In return, they very much loved him. One woman who had a great deal of love for him is Floribeth Mora Diaz, a simple mother and grandmother who loves God and his Church.

In April of 2011, she became quite ill, losing feeling in her left leg and constantly vomiting. After seeing several doctors and undergoing near-endless tests, it was determined that she had an inoperable, untreatable brain aneurism. She was basically told to go home and to prepare for death. As soon as they were able, her family had a priest come to give her Extreme Unction (Anointing of the Sick). She called her family together to give them some last "instructions" and she wept and prayed in pain for three days, continuing to take medicine that the doctor prescribed.

On Divine Mercy Sunday that year, Pope John II was beatified in a ceremony in Rome that was televised worldwide. Mora wanted to watch the ceremony and asked her husband not to give her the sleeping pills the night before so that she would wake up for the morning ceremony. Despite her instructions, however, her husband did give her the pills.

Mora tells us that in the morning, she heard a voice tell her, "Get up," and she awoke. As she took hold of her surroundings, she looked around her room and found that no one was there. But Diaz knew she heard the voice.

She then looked at a special newspaper edition of La Nacion that had been given to her about the beatification ceremony and which had a picture of Pope John Paul II on the cover. She indicates that she then heard the voice again and that it was coming from the picture itself. The voice told her, "Get up and do not be afraid."

Mora got up and said, "Yes sir."

Mora then relates that after that moment, she improved tremendously. She said, "I felt a renewed spirit, a peace in me. I no longer felt that fatigue. I felt strong." She had also woken up right on time, and Mora watched the beatification ceremony on television. She remembers praying, asking then Blessed John Paul II to intercede for her and to bring her healing. She also says that every night she prayed, "Lord, I have faith; but grow my faith, Lord, because I am afraid. John Paul, pray for me."

Mora tells how she went back to the doctors and they were baffled in total amazement that they could no longer find any sign of the aneurism; upon reviewing new scans, it was if it was never there.

She also tells of how she went to visit a relic (a droplet of John Paul's blood) when it came to Costa Rica. She brought flowers to thank him, still keeping the healing low-key. But when she found a website created to honor the future saint, she told her story of how he was responsible for her healing. News of her story soon reached the Vatican and officials became interested and invited Mora to have more tests on her pre- and post-aneurism conditions.

She had a second set while in Costa Rica and then a third set of tests when she was called to Rome.

These tests, along with her original medical records, showed how great of a miracle it actually was, astonishing skeptics. Her healing miracle was used to bring on the canonization of St. John Paul II. Mora, now very well-known, says, "As I said from the first day, don't look at this woman who is here. I am not the important one. What is important here is what God worked in me. Look at me and believe in God. Because I was on the edge of dying, and here I am now, talking with you. So believe in God. You have before you a healing. If you don't believe in this, in what can we believe?"

"Jesus said to him, 'Have you believed because you have seen me? Blessed are those who have not seen and yet believe'" (Jn 20:29).

St. John Paul II, pray for us.

ST. JUNIPERO SERRA: FOUNDING FATHER OF THE UNITED STATES

By Deacon Marty McIndoe

On September 23, 2015, Pope Francis canonized Junipero Serra in the Basilica of the National Shrine of the Immaculate Conception in Washington, DC, making him the first Hispanic American saint.

At this ceremony, Pope Francis said, "He was one of the founding fathers of the United States, a saintly example of the Church's universality and special patron of the Hispanic people of the country. In this way, may all Americans rediscover their own dignity and unite themselves ever more closely to Christ and his Church."

Junipero was born in 1713 on the island of Majorca, off of the Spanish coast, and died in 1784 in Monterrey, California. He was a brilliant man who obtained a doctorate in

Theology and was very comfortable in his Franciscan life as a professor of philosophy at Lullian University in Majorca. But soon, a real desire to spread the Good News to the New World would come over Junipero, and in 1748, he asked his superior for permission to travel to North America and evangelize the native peoples.

Granted the mission, Serra and his brother friars landed in New Spain (present-day Mexico) in 1749. At first, he worked in a school that trained missionaries, but then he decided that he had to go out among the missionaries himself.

During the time Carlos III of Spain expelled the Jesuits from all of the Spanish territories, Junipero Serra's abilities were acknowledged and he became appointed and responsible for building the California missions. Junipero took this role very seriously, pouring all of his being into bringing the Good News to the Native Americans. This wasn't an easy task, as he had met with numerous tribes and had over fifty different languages to deal with! He not only brought the Gospel to them, but also helped them in farming, carpentry, garment making, and other tools to make them self-sufficient.

His love for the Native Americans often brought Junipero into conflict with the Spanish government, which mistreated the Native Americans. There is a notable incident where a Native American was sentenced to death for his part in a raid that destroyed the San Diego Mission and killed several people, including a friar friend of Serra's.

Junipero pleaded with the governor to stop the execution of the murderer. Serra said, "Let the murderer live so he can be saved, which is the purpose of our coming here and the reason for forgiving him." Serra advocated for a more "moderate punishment" so that he could have the opportunity to teach the killer about a higher law, "which orders us to forgive offenses and to prepare him, not for his death, but for eternal life." Serra went on to say that if the Native Americans ever killed him, he would want them to be forgiven.

After a considerable amount of pleading, the governor granted the pardon for the murderer and the others that were part of the raid. Junipero remarked, "Great was our joy when we obtained a general amnesty. Because of our love of God, we set them free, so that they might, having repented, lead better lives."

One more interesting thing is that he took up a collection to help out another Founding Father of the United States, George Washington.

There is significant virtue in the act of standing up for those who cannot stand for themselves.

St. Junipero Serra, pray for us.

PLAYING WITH CANNONS: ST. ALOYSIUS GONZAGA

By Shaun McAfee

Being the son of wealthy and powerful parents in the height of the Renaissance came with a ton of responsibility. It also came with a fair amount of privilege. If that family was among the most famous in Europe, everything you did and said made an impact. Aloysius Gonzaga (1568–1591), better known by his peers as "Luigi," perhaps didn't quite understand that dichotomy at an early age.

His father, Ferrante, was a marquis of the Spanish army occupying the northeastern part of Italy at the time and was frequently gone for war councils and battles all over the known world. He loved his firstborn, Luigi, and wanted to make a military man out of him, and so resolved to have the boy come along on a campaign. Martha, who prayed that her son would become a religious, all but refused the request, but eventually relented. Little Luigi went to war at about six years old.

The boy was overjoyed to join his dad on one of these adventures and, to hallmark the occasion, the marquis gave him a toy gun. Toys were different back then—don't mistake this as a run-of-the-mill wooden gun. It was more like a mini hand cannon! Taking real beads and gun power, it was a real weapon if used properly. His father gave him one rule: only use when supervised.

And like kids usually do, he took that rule and threw it in the garbage.

Remembering how his father taught him to reload, he did his best and took aim at the stack of hay in the barracks. *BLAMM!* Luigi loaded far too much gunpowder and nearly took his hand—or arm—completely off.

Ferrante knew he had to punish the usually well-mannered boy, and he did. What would most kids do? They try again! Oh, but Luigi wasn't like most kids. He was a marvel of uniqueness. Only he would choose to go from toy hand cannon to real cannon. He was bent on regaining his repute at any cost.

In the middle of the night, Luigi got out of bed, got himself dressed, and snuck into the ammo bunker. Emerging with a ball that he could hardly lift, he made it to the gunpowder cache and grabbed enough for a single attempt.

"WAKE UP! WAKE UP! PREPARE FOR BATTLE!"

The entire camp awoke in confusion to the noise of a heavy, loud boom, thinking the enemy had somehow penetrated their lines and was firing their own equipment on them! But confusion turned to astonishment when they found the little boy, nearly dead and concussed, lying next to the cannon—he took the full brunt of the recoil to the chest. Rushing to the scene armed with his men, Ferdinand found not only that it was his son who had fired the cannon but that the recoil had not killed him. In fact, the boy was almost completely unharmed.

What was Ferrante to do? Luigi went unpunished only because the multitude of soldiers admired the little child and talked the marquis out of any further action. They absolutely loved him.

As amusing as the story is, it marked a turning point for the future saint. From then on, he resolved to never be disobedient again. Indeed, he resolved to never sin again. And from then on, his reputation for piety became world famous. He almost never spoke unless it was with the utmost respect, and he achieved an utter perfection in self-mastery when met with a hint of temptation. This once took the eye of King Philip of Spain. One day, the king found humor in realizing that the young man at court never once made eye contact with women in the dining hall.

If he was not a perfect child, St. Aloysius Gonzaga is nonetheless known to be one of the most pious, sinless examples of a Christian life, such that cause for his canonization was sought immediately after his death at just twenty-three. His life changed after firing that cannon, doubtless realizing that his survival was a miracle. From then on, the only army he wanted to serve was the one battling the spiritual realm.

It is truly gratitude that frees us from sin.

St. Aloysius Gonzaga, pray for us.

THE ACTIVE PACIFISM OF ST. MARTIN OF TOURS

By Shaun McAfee

Before he became the bishop of Tours, Martin of Tours (316–397) was a young Roman cavalry soldier from Gaul. He served an unusually long term in the Roman ranks and was immensely influential among his peers. Therefore, whatever he did made a huge mark on the army, especially when those actions were in the service of the Caesar, everyone gave their closest attention. His later biographer Sulpicius Severus recorded a courageous story.

For their valiant service in battle against multiple recent campaigns in Gaul, Martin and his troops were given a salary bonus and honorifics dispensed in a ceremony by Caesar Julian himself. The warriors were called up to receive their reward, one by one, in the usual way until Martin's turn came.

He was a recent convert and was convinced that God

was asking him to be a different kind of soldier: a soldier in God's army.

Therefore, the senior soldier thought it would be a suitable time for applying for his discharge, for he did not think that it would be honest for him to take the bonus if he was not going to fight. Knowing that there was another battle the very next morning, he said to the Caesar, "I have been your soldier up to now. Let me now be God's. Let someone who is going to fight have your bonus. I am Christ's soldier."

These words put the tyrant, whose parents were Christians, into a rage, and he said that it was from fear of the battle that was to be fought the next day that he wanted to quit the service, not from religious motives. But Martin was undaunted. And in fact, he stood all the firmer when the emperor and his entourage tried to frighten him. "If it is put down to cowardice," he said, "and not to faith, I will stand unarmed in front of the battle line tomorrow and I will go unscathed through the enemy's columns in the name of the Lord Jesus, protected by the sign of the Cross instead of by shield and helmet."

His words confronted the Caesar, but left him inspired by Martin's strong faith. Julian relented, allowing him to discharge out of the army after serving twenty-five years. Martin left the military and embraced the monastic lifestyle, settling in the town of Poitiers. Martin's reputation for holiness increased and he soon came to the attention of the saintly and beloved bishop Hilary of Poitiers (310–368). Upon Hilary's death in 368, the people wanted someone special to take his place, and they quickly agreed it should be Martin. Martin had no interest in the episcopacy and wanted to remain a monk, but "once again he would be obliged to do something he had not wanted to do: he would be a bishop in spite of himself."

When God makes your particular vocation certain, trust in him to enable even your judges to acquiesce what he has set in front of you.

St. Martin of Tours, pray for us.

"I CAN DIE NOW": ST. MONICA

By Shaun McAfee

Before he changed the way Christians think of studying God, and pretty much synthesized Christology completely in one simple three-hundred scroll collection, St. Augustine of Hippo was a classic bad boy of the fourth century. He came from wealth. He was great in school, even though he put forth a meager effort. He was a common thief, squandered his thoughts and study on secular things, and was promiscuous, a lover of the pleasures of the flesh. Oh, he also disliked the Christian faith.

Meanwhile, his mother prayed. She counseled him, though he did not listen. She persisted to preach the Christian faith to him but got his most polite shoulder. Finally, she committed the entire hope of his conversion to the Lord and prayed for his change of heart and mind in silence. It took endurance only a mother is capable of, and over time, he did change. After reading the life of St. Anthony of the Desert, he converted and was baptized by St. Ambrose on the Easter Vigil in AD 387.

With acclaim and joy, a few months after Augustine's conversion, Monica (331–387) remarked to her son, "There was indeed one thing for which I wished to wait in this life, and that was that I might see you a Catholic before I died. My God has exceeded this abundantly, so that I see you despising all earthly happiness, for you have been made his servant. What am I doing here?"

Her life's wish realized, Monica died at the age of fifty-six. Never, ever, quit praying for your children and godchildren.

St. Monica, pray for us.

ST. GENEVIEVE
AND THE HUNS

By Shaun McAfee

A century after St. Denis walked with his head in his hands, literally, through the city of Paris after being beheaded by Roman occupiers of Paris, Geneviève (419–512) was born. She was religious from an early age and was known for acts of piety and charity. After her parents died, she moved to Paris to live with her grandmother. Being known for her strict moral conduct and unafraid to protect others of like mind, the bishop of Paris asked Geneviève to look after the consecrated virgins in the city. She received visions of saints and angels and was known for her holiness.

In 451, Attila invaded Gaul. The main target of the leader of the Huns was all the treasure his army could plunder. With this singular goal, he marched his massive army towards Paris. At this time, Paris had a perfect defensive advantage: huge, thick walls, and being surrounded by water. But the Huns were famous for their hellish onslaught of cities thought to be impregnable.

News of the Huns' imminent arrival sent the Parisians into a panicked mass exodus. However, the holy woman Geneviève rallied the people together in the city and urged them to pray for hours (which became known as a "prayer marathon") and perform penances so that God might protect the Christian city. Suddenly, for no known reason, the Huns changed direction and instead marched down the Rhineland, sacking Reims, Mainz, Strasbourg, Cologne, Worms, and Trier instead.

Thirteen years later, another conqueror approached the city of Paris. The Germanic king Childeric I besieged the city. The saintly Geneviève acted as an intermediary between the city and the army that surrounded the city completely. She collected food for the prisoners and eventually convinced Childeric to release them.

She is a reminder that while sometimes we are blessed to receive miracles from God, at all times we have to use the wit and wisdom he gave us.

St. Geneviève, pray for us.

POPE LEO MEETS ATTILA THE HUN

By Shaun McAfee

If the name of Attila denotes fear and conjures images of devastation in modern times, his advancement on cities of antiquity caused all unimaginable alarm. When Attila sacked a city, those cities were often unrecognizable after his army took what they wanted and scourged what remained. With all the energy that enabled him to seize much of Northern Europe, he decided to invade the Italian peninsula in AD 452.

Sacking city after city, driving Italians to the coastal lagoons, one of which would become the city of Venice, Attila was finally halted by the Po River. Not unpassable, Attila had already crossed major rivers such as the Rhine and the Danube, but here his forces were met by an envoy sent from Rome.

Emperor Valentinian III sent a mix of leadership to greet

the invader in the hopes of negotiating some sensible solution for peace. He sent high ranking civilian officials, Gennadius Avienus and Trigetius. For an extra measure, he also sent the bishop of Rome, Leo I (400–461).

Pope Leo received reports about the march of the Huns. Attila had great plans for sacking Rome, but was willing to listen to the envoy. Negotiations were wavering, and history does not record what the great pope said to the great conqueror, but after the papal visit, Attila's army broke camp and marched away. Leo had saved Rome and the entire Italian peninsula. The prominent Christian historian and contemporary of Augustine of Hippo Prosper of Aquitaine makes a small mention about the meeting of Attila and Pope Leo but gives all the credit to Leo for the successful negotiations.

Leo reminds us that the shrewd leadership of religious in the secular realm is every bit as important as their discerning leadership in the spiritual realm.

St. Leo the Great, pray for us.

LEO AND GENSERIC

By Shaun McAfee

Also known as Geiseric, Genseric was the Arian ruler of the destructive Vandals. Arianism is the heretical belief that denies the divinity of Christ as being of the same substance as God the Father. The name of the Vandals precedes their reputation: they were great looters, destroyers of art, and wrecked the monuments of whomever they overcame and whatever cities they sacked.

In the middle of summer in the year AD 455, the Vandals approached Rome, and it was there that the saintly Pope Leo marched out to meet them just as he did Attila the Hun.

Historians and biographers recount a consistent episode where Leo the Great received Genseric with peace and urged him to consider his actions carefully: murder, rape, loot, and destroy, or simply conquer, rule in peace, and enjoy the spoils of victory. Leo likely wanted nothing more than the safekeeping of the many treasures and artifacts within the walls of Rome but would be satisfied with the simple safety of innocent families, ranchers, and laborers in the city.

Leo's mission was partly successful compared to his dealings with Attila. Although Genseric agreed to loot the city and not destroy it, the Vandals did not stay and some peace was enjoyed. And entire success or not, it required incredible guts to ask a nomadic ruler such as Genseric to not destroy your city. Leo the Great did it twice.

Diplomacy is an invaluable skill for every Christian, not just popes.

St. Leo the Great, pray for us.

WHY ARE SOME SAINTS NOT ON THE CALENDAR?

By Shaun McAfee

This is a fair question that comes up often. It's also a question that is laced with a certain unawareness, because the fact is that every saint has a feast day, sometimes known as an optional memorial. That day is typically the day that particular saint died, but some have been placed on a specific day for one reason or another. And on that day there may be up to fifteen (or more!) different saints as memorial. The General Roman Calendar of 1969 shifted some feast days and omitted some historical, albeit not universal, feast days.

That there is a Roman calendar implies something important: the existence of other calendars. It's important to remember that the Church is universal, but the liturgy is not. The liturgy is the way we worship, and so it makes sense that the Eastern Rite may celebrate the lives of saints that are not on the Roman calendar and that some would be shared.

Therefore, saints like Irene of Chrysovalantou might have a feast day or memorial, but they will only be a feast day or memorial on a specific calendar.

It's not just a difference of East and West, though. Religious orders—or institutes of consecrated life—have what are called "congregational calendars," and these may contain completely different feast days and memorials centric to that order's liturgy.

So, if you find that your saint is not given the status of a major feast day—especially that super hipster saint that nobody knows about—you are welcome to celebrate that day in agreement with the liturgy.

POPE GELASIUS SAYS NO MORE

By Shaun McAfee

Although tensions were high between the Catholic leadership and the Roman rulers, there came a time when there was established a mutual understanding that the Catholic Church was actually the antithesis to the enormous instability in Rome and the Christian world. Close to two centuries after Constantine legalized Christianity and the Roman Empire was split between powers in Constantinople and Ravenna, new aggressors emerged. One of these was Odoacer, a barbarian ruler. With successful conquests on the Italian peninsula, he became the first king of Italy.

Odoacer was a religious man and, interestingly for an Arian of his time, held good relations with the Trinitarian Catholic Church. It was even more interesting when he was driven to, in a way, rule alongside the Catholic Church, which was actively engaged in putting an end to the greatly divisive heresy.

Twenty years after Odoacer's rebellion, Pope St. Gelasius (r. 492–496) formulated a new political norm in the West known as the "Two Powers." Gelasius wrote to the Eastern emperor Anastasius I. He explained his position: "There are two powers, august Emperor, by which this world is chiefly ruled, namely the sacred authority of the priests and the royal power. Of these, that of the priests is the more weighty, since they have to render an account for even the kings of men in the divine judgment."

Pope Gelasius's letter to the emperor stands as a milestone in the development of the relationship between the ecclesial and civil authorities. St. Ambrose of Milan, a tremendous influence on Christian thought at the time, had advocated that the emperor, if Christian, was not above rebuke from the Church in certain matters. But Gelasius's position went further and argued that ecclesial power is higher and more important than civil power because the Church answers to God for the actions of men.

In the short-term, this created a (mostly healthy) tension in the West between the Church and the civil political power, in contrast to the East, where the Church was subservient to the emperors' policy of *caesaro-papism*.

Gelasius, when we think of it, was daring to make such statements. He put his life, and the lives of non-Arian worshipers, at stake when he took such a bold position directly to the ruler.

St. Gelasius, pray for us.

HISTORY'S TURNING POINT: ST. CLOTILDA AND THE CONVERSION AND BAPTISM OF CLOVIS

By Shaun McAfee

St. Clotilda (474–545) is one of the most important saints in the entire history of the Church, but is sadly not well-known outside of France.

Born a Burgundian princess, Clotilda was pledged in marriage to Clovis of the Franks to strengthen the alliance between the two peoples who had a history of brutal warfare and stubborn politics. They married in the late fifth century, and Clovis was also a few years senior to Clotilda.

Clotilda was Catholic, despite the fact that most Burgundians were Arian. Raised by her Catholic mother, Clotilda held strongly to the Faith and prayed constantly for Clovis's conversion. On several occasions, she also tried to reason with Clovis. She once wrote to him, "The gods whom you worship are no good. They haven't even been able to help themselves, let alone others. They are carved out of stone or wood or some old piece of metal. The very names, which you have given them were the names of men, not gods. You ought instead to worship him who created at a word and out of nothing heaven, the earth, the sea."

Clovis was not swayed by Clotilda's reasoning and gave a weak response. He contended that the Christian God "can do nothing, and, what is more, there is no proof that he is God at all."

Clovis's obstinacy only motivated Clotilda all the more. She continued to argue with, reason with, and, most importantly, pray fervently for her husband. One prayer was answered when Clovis agreed to allow the baptism of their firstborn son, but the boy died shortly after receiving the sacrament.

Clovis viewed his son's death as proof that Clotilda's God was false, arguing that if he had been dedicated in the names of the pagan gods, the child would have surely lived. Clotilda answered with unshakable faith, "I give thanks to Almighty God, the Creator of all things, who has not found me completely unworthy, for he has deigned to welcome to his Kingdom the child conceived in my womb. I am not at all cast down in my mind because of what has happened, for I know that my child, who was called away from this world in his white baptismal robes, will be nurtured in the sight of God."

Soon, Clovis would lead his army in a campaign against

another Germanic tribe known as the Alemanni, who obstructed the consolidation of his power in Gaul. In the pivotal battle of the campaign, the Alemanni gained the lead and Clovis recognized the enormity of the situation. He was on the edge of despair, and Clovis reached out to the heavens, invoking Clotilda's God—the God he had refused and blamed for his misfortune—as one final act towards propitiousness. And almost immediately the fight turned to Clovis's favor, and before the hour was over, the Franks had defeated the Alemanni.

When he returned home, Clovis told Clotilda what happened on the battlefield, and she quickly dispatched a message to Bishop Remigius—with whom she had kept near-constant contact—to come and instruct Clovis in the Faith so he could receive baptism.

Remigius, future saint and bishop of Reims, came immediately. During his baptismal preparation, Clovis still was concerned when he considered how his warriors would react. His concern was that his troops might overthrow him for rejecting their ancestral gods or that they might allow his conversion but not accept the Faith themselves, which would cause division in the tribe.

So Clovis mustered his army and informed them of his intention to convert and proceeded to ask for their honest opinion. They not only agreed, but the entire army asked for baptism!

At their request, on Christmas Day in the year 496, the prayers of Clotilda, Remigius, and Geneviève were answered. Clovis, King of the Franks, was baptized in Reims, along with three thousand Frankish warriors. Historians report that the cathedral in Reims was so packed with people that the cleric holding the sacred chrism could not get through the crowd—and a dove descended with a vial of oil to Remigius, who took the oil and anointed Clovis. This very same holy oil was used for the next 1,300 years to anoint the kings of France.

Clovis went on to work in establishing a strong relationship with the Church in several ways, such as instituting reforms and recognizing the independence of the Church in his territory.

Clotilda's story went on as the kingdom of the Franks, according to custom, was divided among the sons of Clovis upon the great king's death. But the brothers quarreled, and Queen Clotilda witnessed bloody infighting among her sons over Gaul. The saintly wife of Clovis outlived him by thirty-four years, and for decades, she spent her time financing the construction of churches and monasteries and living a penitential life of prayer, first in Paris and then at the Shrine of St. Martin of Tours.

By her prayers, exemplary Christian living, and wifely vocation, Clotilda changed the course of Church history. The event is so important that Pope St. John Paul II traveled to France in 1996 to celebrate the 1,500th anniversary of Clovis's baptism.

St. Clotilda, pray for us.

GREGORY HIDES IN A CAVE, INSTEAD OF BEING POPE

By Shaun McAfee

It must have been difficult to be named Pelagius in the sixth century. Just a hundred years earlier, a British monk with the namesake introduced a damaging heresy that twisted the Christian doctrine of Original Sin, declaring that it did not taint the human nature and that the will of man could still choose between good and evil and obtain paradise without divine grace. The name Pelagius, however, was the name of two popes at the end of the sixth century. One of them was the favorite of Emperor Justinian, and he was installed with little argument from the clergy and without an election. Three popes later, Pelagius II, who was a great diplomat, was elected, but died when a severe flood of the Tiber in 590 caused a terrible plague.

After the death of Pope Pelagius II, a pope of a new kind was elected: a monk named Gregorius (540–604). The bishops wanted to try something different and elect a man who was not interested in the politics of Rome or Constantinople and could completely devote himself to resurrecting the charitable office of the bishop of Rome.

Gregory returned to Rome where he was from, but had no idea that the clergy had elected him bishop. Not only undesirous of local politics, Gregory had no interest in the papacy and, after his diplomatic adventures, wanted nothing more than to return to his simple monastic life.

He wrote a letter to the emperor, asking him to repudiate the election, but the emperor refused.

So he did what any normal person would do: ran to a cave in the middle of nowhere as fast as he could.

Gregory fled the city and hid in a cave for three days, believing another man would be chosen during his absence. Eventually realizing that the monastery was not God's plan for his life, he agreed to assume the papacy.

He went on to become one of the most influential popes of all time, igniting a new standard for papal piety. There's not a lot of sense in being afraid of what God is asking us to do: if he asks it, we'll surely be happy.

Pope St. Gregory the Great, pray for us.

ST. LAWRENCE AND THE GRILL

By Shaun McAfee

A little more than two hundred years after Jesus was crucified, Lawrence was ordained a deacon by Pope St.
Sixtus II. He became a saint, but not before he endured a
thrilling and miraculous martyrdom, which also involved
some hilarity.

Lawrence was one of a handful of deacons in Rome at the
time, and he was genuinely upset when he learned that a
number of the other deacons of Rome were being martyred
but not him. "Why would God want others to die for their
Faith but not me?" he wondered.

Emperor Valerian had ordered the death of all Rome's
bishops, priests, and deacons. The prefect who carried out
the order knew that, as a deacon, Lawrence had charge of the
Church's money. So he made an offer to Lawrence: "I'll let
you go free if you will turn the money over to me."

Lawrence agreed to bring the Church's treasures to the prefect. "The Church is very rich, but it will take me a few days," he said.

Released to carry out his promise, Lawrence distributed the Church's goods and wealth among the poor. He then gathered the city's lame, its blind, and its beggars. On the third day, he appeared before the prefect.

"You wanted the Church's treasure; well, look no further."

The prefect was enraged as Lawrence explained that these poor people would someday have new bodies and live for all eternity in paradise. The treasure of the Holy Spirit was hidden in them as if in jars of clay—"a true treasure," he assured the prefect.

Unamused, the prefect ordered a slow and painful death for Lawrence. On August 10, 258, Lawrence was tortured by having his arms dislocated and was then laid upon a grill and slowly roasted to death. During his ordeal, he is said to have remarked, "Turn me over, I'm done on this side." He was so calm that the pagans who observed were greatly astonished and impressed.

Close to a hundred years later, his story was so well known that the famous Bishop Ambrose of Milan wrote about him, and so did others. By then, Emperor Constantine had long since built a chapel in his memory. Later, popes built other memorials, and these became Rome's Church of San Lorenzo.

St. Lawrence, pray for us.

"NON NISI TE, DOMINE": ST. THOMAS AQUINAS

By Shaun McAfee

Thomas Aquinas (1225–1274) loved his religious order and the monastic lifestyle. He enjoyed a quiet life of prayer and teaching other priests in the Faith, solely desiring to be a simple monastic Dominican priest. But with God's gifts of an outstanding mind for philosophy and such a wit for communicating the Faith, he spent much of his time teaching and writing, often at the request of his superiors.

It was towards the end of his life that he was asked to summarize the Catholic faith in a single volume of concise, convincing arguments. This became the *Summa Theologiae*, the brick and mortar of the next eight hundred years of theological study in seminaries and in the university. And though it was intended to be a "summary" of the Faith, it is still regarded as one of the most thorough vindications of the Catholic faith. There's nearly no question or subject St. Thomas doesn't address.

Divided into three parts, the work consists of 38 tracts, 631 questions, about 3,000 articles, and 10,000 objections and their answers; needless to say, it was an unfathomably exhausting project. It required countless hours and days to get just right, and he couldn't ignore his priestly responsibilities either.

Months into the project, after writing on the Eucharist, St. Thomas received a supreme gift: he entered into an ecstasy. He heard a voice from the crucifix nearby on the altar say, "You have written well of me, Thomas. What reward would you have?"

St. Thomas's reply was, "Non nisi te, Domine. Non nisi te." (Nothing but you, Lord.)

The *Summa* was an achievement of achievements, and still, Thomas wanted nothing more than God. Not praise, not a day off; just the Lord. Our achievements, big and small, will never satisfy us completely. And we don't need to write three thousand articles to learn that.

St. Thomas Aquinas, pray for us.

FIRM BELIEF:
ST. TARCISIUS

By Shaun McAfee

The Roman Martyrology records the names and some-times a short story of those who have died, from Rome to the furthest stretches of the Faith. But of the many tens of thousands, there are so few stories because few traditions of the deaths survived. One of the heroic and miraculous stories that did survive was that of the young boy Tarcisius (263–275).

He was an altar server, probably being groomed for the deaconate and priesthood, and despite his age, he held close to his Christian faith, even though he heard stories of the ongoing persecutions against Christians.

He was willing to die for his faith, and being a servant in the Mass meant he would serve Christ to others, literally, as he would deliver the Eucharist to those who could not make it to Mass. This included those who were imprisoned, those who were condemned to death for their faith, and also those who would have a Eucharistic service in hiding.

One day, there was no deacon to send with the precious Hosts, and so Tarcisius was the only acolyte available. He left without question.

In the streets of Rome, he was stopped by a group of boys his age who wanted him to play games with them, but he refused, explaining he had business to tend to.

"Oh? Christian boy?" One of them sneered, "It is that you think you are too good to play with us?"

"Not at all," said Tarcisius. "I have something to deliver and must be on my way."

"Well, show us what it is! What is the big secret, Christian boy?"

"It is no business of yours," said Tarcisius, looking each of the boys squarely in the eye. "Now step aside and make way."

Rather than step aside, the pagan boys closed their circle around Tarcisius, and as they did, they picked up heavy sticks and rocks from the ground. One of them shouted, "I bet he's carrying the Christian Mysteries!"

"Are you, Christian boy?" demanded another. "Show us!"

Tarcisius, clutching his precious cargo to his chest made a dash for what looked like an opening in the circle, but he was not quick enough. The mob of boys closed in around him, and they began to club him with stones and heavy sticks. Tarcisius did not cry out but quietly prayed, ever clutching the Blessed Sacrament to his chest.

He went down under the blows nearly dead when a fellow Christian came along and drove away the mob.

The legendary martyrdom passes tradition that Tarcisius

died on the way back from his severe beating. But even when his body was laid in front of the elders, his hands were still clutching strong to the Eucharist.

Tarcisius believed so firmly in the Real Presence that he was willing to give his own body to protect the body of his Savior.

St. Tarcisius, pray for us.

SOME PEOPLE CHANGE, OTHERS ARE REFINED: ST. PHILIP NERI

By Shaun McAfee

I f there was ever a practical joker saint, it was Philip Neri (1515–1595). His life almost came to an end at an early age when he used to joke with animals. Once, as a young boy, he tried to climb onto an ox to ride the beast and it toppled over onto him. That's about one thousand pounds, solid, any day of the week. His parents actually thought their dear little "pippin" was dead. But he lived and turned things around, giving his life to the Lord and only making more calculated practical jokes from then on.

And these calculated jokes were pretty clever. Aside from showing up to the house of one of his parishioners with half of his beard shaved off, Philip also took the liberty of adding humor to his homilies.

When a scholarly bishop who had been used to the stoic seriousness of his office attended Philip's Mass, he was in for a treat. To lighten the ambiance, Philip committed every possible error in pronunciation during that homily. *EE-you-kerist, ay-pow-stle, bih-bull, disk-ay-pull, hereh-say,* he probably could have been censured for his clear lack of education, but nothing he said was heretical—just ridiculously mispronounced.

The crowd wasn't sure if they should laugh or remain silent. How Philip Neri was able to keep composure is beyond our comprehension, but he maintained his mispronouncing character throughout the entire sermon.

St. Neri often reminds us that humor and joy are intertwined.

St. Philip Neri, pray for us.

"I DARE YOU TO TRY": ST. SCHOLASTICA

By Shaun McAfee

Scholastica (480–543) was the twin sister of St. Benedict, founder of the Benedictine Order, and together, they are the founders of Western Monasticism for men and women. They had the custom of visiting each other once a year in which they would spend one whole day together glorifying God in prayer and adoration. They would share meals and converse about the joys that awaited them in heaven.

On one visit, Benedict was finishing his dinner and readying himself to head back to his monastery. It was a clear night with no clouds, only stars and moonlight filled the air. Scholastica stopped him and said, "I beg you. Do not leave me this night so that we may talk until morning more about the joys of heavenly life." But he responded, "What are you talking about, my sister? Under no circumstances can I stay outside my cell."

Upon this, she leaned her head into her hands in prayer, prostrate . . . on the dinner table!

According to her biographers, when she lifted her head, "there broke forth such powerful lightning and thunder and such a flood of rain that neither the venerable Benedict nor the brothers with him could set foot outside the door of the place where they were sitting."

Benedict then told her, "May God have mercy on you, my sister. Why have you done this?"

And she replied to him, "See, I asked you, and you would not listen to me. So I asked my Lord, and he has listened to me. Now then, go, if you can. Leave me, and go back to the monastery."

She basically said, "I dare you to try."

Needless to say, the weather didn't get any better. Benedict remained with his sister for the remainder of the night, and Scholastica scored a million Catholic practical joke points with the assistance of God the Father.

If the answer is no, maybe ask God what the correct answer is (but be okay if the answer is still no).

Saints Scholastica and Benedict, pray for us.

PAINTING A SAINT?: ST. BENEDICT JOSEPH LABRE

By Shaun McAfee

Saints give us the most remarkable quotes, feats of bravery, and imitations of Christ. And sometimes, the stories that have been passed down are, upon examination, just a little odd. Such is the story of the painting—the only one, in fact—of St. Benedict Joseph Labre (1748–1783), a French Catholic who, sort of, just wanted to be left alone.

From an early age he expressed a love for Christ and a holy life. He wanted to study nothing but the saints and the Scriptures, so much so that his uncle, who was overseeing his education, had to force him to understand Latin and other broad subjects—which were still meaningful and included in the requirements of a candidate for Holy Orders. Benedict never resisted.

As he turned eighteen years old, it was clear to him that he had a religious calling, and much to the dismay of his parents whom he was still living with, he set out to join the most austere monastery possible: he went sixty miles, barefoot, to La Trappe.

They did not accept him. Like his parents warned, he was too young.

So he tried the Carthusians, and later the Cistercians, but rather than questioning his age, they questioned his fitness for community life. In view of his eccentric grace, nobody agreed he could live in a solitary cell. Benedict never resisted. "God's will be done," he said, and left.

He left for Rome, going the entire way on alms. And it was in the Eternal City that he realized that he wanted to spend his time becoming a perpetual pilgrim, visiting the shrines all over Europe: Switzerland, Italy, Germany, France, Spain, Loretto, Venice, Assisi, Bari, Einsiedeln, Aix, the Compostela, and anywhere else his feet and the Holy Spirit might take him.

Along the way, he continued his austerity. He accepted no bed, ever, and if he was given money and not food, he passed it on. When he slept, it was on the open ground. And so, wherever he went, he appeared to passersby not as a saint but as just another destitute man. Such was the case when in Italy, he fell asleep in prayer in a church and a man had an idea: he would paint the portrait of a homeless man. Brilliant? Time would tell.

For many years, Benedict resided in Rome, and there he became known as the "beggar of Rome," while the random painter became the famous Boroque artist Antonio Cavallucci. Those who knew Benedict's likeness well instantly recognized him in the painting, which became perhaps the artist's most distributed work.

Preserve holiness, however the Holy Spirit leads you to do so.

St. Benedict Joseph Labre, pray for us.

WHAT IS THE PROCESS FOR CANONIZATION?

By Shaun McAfee

"*Santo subito!*" may be cried by all when a particularly beloved person of God dies, but canonizations do not happen quickly and do not happen without a diligent investigation. As we explored elsewhere in this book, the process for a canonization had matured over the two-thousand-year history of the Church, and continues to advance. Here are the basic steps involved.

The process starts not with the Vatican at all but with the people of God. According to the Congregation for the Cause of Saints, "The petitioner advances the cause of canonization. Any member of the People of God or any group of the faithful recognized by ecclesiastical authority can exercise this function."[3] It is the responsibility of the petitioner

---

[3]   Cardinal Pietro Palazzini (1983), *New Laws for the Causes of Saints*, 1(a).

and the legitimately appointed postulator, at least five years after the death of a person, to gather all required documents for the petition to the Holy See. Sometimes, a pope waives the five-year rule, as in the case of Saints Theresa of Calcutta and Pope John Paul II.

After the five years have concluded, the bishop of the diocese in which the individual died can petition the Holy See to allow the initialization of a Cause for Beatification and Canonization. If there is no objection, the Congregation for the Doctrine of the Faith issues the permission, or *nihil obstat* (nothing stands in the way), which is communicated to the initiating bishop. Once a cause has begun, the individual is called a Servant of God. This title precedes, in most cases, the birth name of the individual. Such as Servant of God Karol Wojtyła or the Servant of God Pope John Paul II.

Over the course of the subsequent years, writings, statements, testimonies, and all related facts are compiled, known as the *Acta*, and provided to a diocesan tribunal for judgment and the bishop's ultimate decision to proceed with the cause. This is the *Informative Process*.

Next, this *Positio* is taken to the Relator, appointed by the Congregation for the Cause of Saints, who ensures the completeness and organization of the cause is properly prepared according to norms. From there, the theological commission votes on the cause, and if the decision is affirmative, the recommendation of a Decree of Heroic Virtues is sent to the Holy Father, whose judgment is final. If the cause is approved by the pope, the individual is given the title of Venerable.

A single attributed miracle invoked by the venerable's

intercession, then, is the remaining step before the beatification of the venerable. If this happens, the miracle is brought forth for investigation in the diocese where it is alleged to have occurred, not in the diocese of the cause (if not the same). The diocese of the candidate miracle conducts an expansive investigation, scientific and theological. These investigators have extremely high standards and will not halt to find an examiner that can prove an alleged miracle was, in fact, a natural event. Therefore, the task of the investigators, together, is to determine if the miracle is legitimate and if it is rightly attributed to the intercession of the specific individual. This decision is sent to the Holy See.

The Congregation of the Cause of Saints, then, makes an arduous and comprehensive investigation of the proposed miracle. The decision is forwarded to the supreme pontiff. It's important to know that in cases of martyrdom, the miracle required for beatification can be waived—since martyrdom is understood as a miracle of grace. If this is the case, the Congregation would investigate and decide that the death of the Servant of God is a true martyrdom, resulting in a Decree of Martyrdom by the Holy Father. If a miracle is approved by the pope, the venerable can by beatified in a rite, giving the person the title of Blessed.

Blesseds, then, may by publicly venerated at the local or regional level. The restriction of veneration is usually to those dioceses or religious institutes closely associated with the person's life. This is a disciplinary norm, and the reason for it is that beatification is not considered an infallible papal act, and so it is not yet appropriate that the entire Church give liturgical veneration to the blessed.

From here, a second miracle must undergo the intensive process, the same as the first. Sometimes, a third is also advanced. If approved, the blessed may be canonized as a saint. Universal veneration is authorized and Masses, offices of prayer, and other acts of veneration, may now be offered throughout the universal Church. If the saint has some universal appeal, he is usually added to the general calendar of the Church as a feast, memorial, or optional memorial.

So when you find yourself chanting *"SANTO SUBITO! SANTO SUBITO!"* ("immediate saint!") in the streets of Rome after a pope dies, or anywhere else in the world, be sure to remember the process involves an army of advocates, scrutinizing investigations, and a lengthy approval process at multiple levels.

INSANE, OR JUST A GOOD EVANGELIST? ST. JOHN BOSCO

By Shaun McAfee

John Bosco (1815–1888) was a restless servant of God. He had a zeal for all souls, but especially for youth, which led him to master many "unpriestly" skills such as juggling, acrobatics, and magic tricks. He understood how to capture the hearts of young people with inspiration and playfulness.

His reputation grew in Turin, Italy, where he taught and loved among a large group of young men, and helped them lead happier, holier lives. His methods were a bit unorthodox from that of his peers, which led a few of his fellow priests to recommend John Bosco to a mental institution for further evaluation and correction.

Bosco knew of their intentions, so he knew just what to do when the priests came to him with a horse and carriage.

He politely waited as the two priests entered into the carriage. When it was his turn to step up, he slammed the door, slapped the horse, and yelled to the carriage driver, "To the asylum! They're expecting them!"

If it brings glory for the kingdom and leads souls to Christ, never substitute its intentions with that of the world. Better yet, never try to trick a holy trickster!

St. John Bosco, pray for us.

ST. CHRISTINA THE ASTONISHING AND THE SMELL OF SIN

By Shaun McAfee

Sin stinks, and there's a saint to prove it! Christina (1150–1224) was a devoted woman whose heart for the lame and destitute brought her to extreme servitude. She was born into a religious family as the youngest of three daughters.

Christina was never in stable health, and throughout her youth, she suffered from sudden and violent seizures. At the age of twenty-one, she suffered from an intense seizure that left her in the clutches of death. It left her motionless and nearly breathless. So much so that it wasn't long after that seizure that the townspeople believed her soul had departed from her body and the people of her hometown of St. Trond, Belgium, commenced with her funeral.

They prepared her for burial and placed her in a coffin.

While her body lay motionless in the coffin, it began to levitate. Higher and higher it flew until it touched the ceiling of the church. Everyone was astonished, and with their jaws wide open, the priest, unphased, ordered Christina's body to return to the coffin, which it did out of obedience to his authority.

As soon her body found its place, she arose fully alive and with more zeal to serve God through prayer and fasting than ever before. Her story fascinated others and she was asked about the levitation. She told the people that the reason she levitated was so that she could escape the foul smell of their sins. With her sobering words, the people of St. Trond sought penance immediately.

She spent the rest of her life praying and fasting for the remission of the sins of others. She died when she was seventy-four years old, and probably smells quite good in heaven.

Sin is real, and sin creates a stench. Pray, through the intercession of St. Christina the Astonishing, that our lives may be an aroma pleasing to the Lord.

St. Christina the Astonishing, pray for us.

ALMOST A POPE TWICE: ST. ROBERT BELLARMINE

By Shaun McAfee

Extraordinary acts of courage are plentiful with the saints. But just as there are many kinds of courage, the saints have demonstrated their courage in many forms. Those who have become our popes are perhaps some of the most extraordinary examples of a certain form of courage. There is no one formula to becoming pope, and no single kind of bishop that becomes pope. At various moments in Church history, the College of Cardinals have enjoyed their free will choice in prayerfully selecting a bishop of Rome.

Ordinarily, individuals selected to be the successor of Peter know in advance during the election process. Also among the ordinary in the election of a pope is the frequent reluctance of an apparent nominee to accept the position. Many popes, such as Leo I (440–461), did not wish to be pope but accepted the position upon further discernment—and went on to perform the office with grace. It seems, when reading the lives of popes who have become saints, that the initial reluctance is their personal measure of their ability to execute the office of supreme pontiff. It is, certainly, to be read with a flavor of supreme humility on their behalf; for sure, the demands of the papal office are tiring, the challenges are endless, and the personal judgment involved for the papacy and the Church as a whole must be immensely intimidating. Still, most of these reluctant nominees eventually agree as a matter of cooperation with the Holy Spirit and the functions of the Church.

But that doesn't mean that every apparent nominee agrees to the office. Even among the saints, there are some who have denied the Chair of St. Peter out of a stricter obedience to their conscience. Such is the case of Robert Cardinal Bellarmine (1542–1621).

The goal of Robert Bellarmine, from an early age, was to be the best parish priest he could. But his gifts of intellect and the exertion of his will were evident from an early age. He knew Virgil's poems by heart and mastered theological concepts despite his parent's lack of funding for a solid education. Almost annually after his ordination, he was promoted or moved throughout Italy because he excelled in task and impact wherever he went, whatever he was ordered to do.

Eventually, though he resisted it, he became a cardinal in 1599 by the immediate selection of Clement VIII at a time when no one wished to assume that responsibility. After this, in somewhat of a reverse order, he became the Cardinal Inquisitor, and then an archbishop. Clement famously remarked of Bellarmine upon receiving the crimson cassock that "the Church and God have not an equal in his learning." The other cardinals and bishops wholeheartedly agreed. When Bellarmine was asked to do something, he did it right.

In 1605, it was the task of the College of Cardinals to elect a new pope. Bellarmine—highly regarded by the College—was quickly the forerunner, but he ensured the vote swung away from him. Alessandro Medici was then elected and became Pope Leo XI. He was pope for twenty-seven days before dying on April 27 of fatigue and the common cold, earning the title, "the Lightning Pope."

The papal conclave resumed once again on May 11, 1605, and Bellarmine was the apparent elect once again, and with significantly more votes. Concluding the day's conclave, he was asked if he would accept the election, since a month earlier he indicated his reluctance.

Bellarmine, nose to the ground in thought, pointed to a lone piece of straw on the ground and said, "If picking up a straw from the ground made me pope, the straw would remain where it was." The votes quickly caused him to fall out of the running. Pope Paul V was elected.

Still, some thought it amusing to guess at the duration of Pope Paul V's reign, many guessing, again, for a short papacy. With confidence, Bellarmine said, "Do not believe it, for he will have a long reign. Sixteen years—he will reign sixteen years." Pope Paul V died in 1621.

"In all your ways acknowledge him, and he will make straight your paths" (Prv 3:6). Though Bellarmine decided against the wishes of the majority of the College, he was ultimately obedient to God and his conscience, both of which require extraordinary courage.

St. Robert Bellarmine, pray for us.

AGAINST ALL ODDS: ST. STEPHEN HARDING

By Shaun McAfee

A young man and his friend left the Sherborne Abbey where they received their childhood education in hopes of seeing the rest of Scotland, Paris, and then Rome. Spending enough time in the Eternal City and all its churches have to offer one's faith, the band of two set foot northward, back to England.

But on the way back, in a remote Burgundy forest where one could hardly make a life, they found a small group of monks living a most arduous lifestyle with their time split between prayer and difficult manual labor. The place was called Molesmes, and so impressed was Stephen Harding (1060–1134) that he elected to stay with the brothers and become a monk in whatever lot awaited them.

Though things were generally good for a time, whatever spirit existed in Molesmes was agreed by the brothers to have departed, and they together travelled to Archbishop Hugh in Lyons for a release, and permission to find a new home. The gentle archbishop and legate to the Holy See agreed and it was done, and the men selected Cîteaux. It wasn't much better. Cîteaux was gloomy, rarely saw the sun, and was positively the worst choice for making a farm. But the monks settled there and were committed to their decision. They made a structure of leaders with Stephen as third-in-charge, a sub-prior.

Funds were scarce, and usually turned away if not in trade for honest labor. The tools used for farming were primitive and often broke; they made little to no success converting the forest-y marsh to an arable plot. As winter settled in, the men had nothing to eat—sometimes for weeks.

When, about six to eight years later, the prior left to return to Molesmes and the other had died, Stephen was elected as his replacement, and he began the tedious work of managing the expenses in order to focus on matters of survival. He made sure that nothing unnecessary was purchased and anything that *was* necessary was not gaudy nor expensive—including the vestments and vessels for Mass.

It was a solid strategy, because soon starvation would face the community at Cîteaux. Stephen Harding asked for a volunteer to visit the nearby market to purchase three horses and three carts and to return with all the means necessary for survival. Reluctant, because he was given three pence to cover all of the logistics, a volunteer set off on the mission impossible.

Upon reaching the city, he informed a friend of his orders and the friend immediately ran away. The hard circumstance almost caused the brother to turn back for Cîteaux, but the friend of the community soon returned with a bundle of money which he received from an older villager on his deathbed.

Despite this wonderful event, the supplies dwindled, numbers of the brothers diminished, and spirits were lacking. To test their grit further, a pestilence broke out and what money they did have was spent trying to save the lives of the monks. But many died anyways—some of them from disease, some of starvation. It seemed clear to Stephen that nothing worse could happen and that the move to Cîteaux was a complete mistake. Feeling pessimistic but steadfast in his faith, he put all of his hope in God, and nobody could predict how dramatically God was about to answer.

Several mornings later, there appeared about thirty men at the priory gate, begging to be admitted to the community.

"We're starving in here," said the future saint.

"We're hungry for the Lord," replied the strangers.

The tired prior let them in. Upon dining with them, he learned that they were all of noble lineage, young, educated, in their prime, and not lacking in piety.

But why did the thirty men desire entry to Cîteaux? It had to do, really, with a single member of the assembly. From the earliest of his memories, he delighted in the consideration of becoming a religious hermit or monk but would not do so unless all of his friends joined him. The men loved their friend and leader greatly and agreed to follow him wherever he went. His name was Bernard, and he would become one of the most influential saints in European history.

Prior Harding, from then on, never was in want of

funding or supplies or novices but kept his mind and will hard pressed on two goals: founding and organizing more monasteries and training the young Bernard of Clairvaux. Within a decade, the Cistercian Order was approved, the constitution was formed, and an advanced system of abbeys, chapters, and provinces were formed. The Cistercian Order became the overwhelming religious influence in France. And his pupil Bernard would go on to become a Doctor of the Church, a major leader in the reform and prevention of schism in the next century of the Church, and the chief preacher for the Second Crusade.

To be a great saint, it doesn't take being the front man— just the one willing to do the dirty work.

St. Stephen Harding, pray for us.

FINALLY A POPE, AND A RECONCILED ANTIPOPE

By Shaun McAfee

In the first half of the third century, the Church managed to elect popes, but those popes found great difficulty in the rapidly changing politics of Rome and from within Christian leadership. In 217, Pope Callixtus I (d. 222) was elected, who had previously served Pope Zephyrinus as a deacon and assistant. But years before this, Callixtus was charged with having started a brawl in a synagogue. For that, he was sent to the labor mines in Sardinia, which nearly killed him before being released by the political leverage Pope Victor I was able to manage with Emperor Commodus's wife, Marcia. Though perhaps by mistake, Victor had left Callixtus off his list of slaves negotiated for release, and the future pope talked the guard into letting him go with the other Christians.

His service to the pope, then, came in whatever capacity

was demanded of him, and since he was quite learned, he aided Pope Zephyrinus in the ongoing intellectual clashes regarding the development of Trinitarian theology. For this, he was opposed by a learned presbyter named Hippolytus.

Hippolytus was a highly influential bishop in Roman Christian politics and opposed Pope Zephyrinus; therefore, he directly opposed the ascendancy of the newly elected Pope Callixtus. Hippolytus so opposed the new pontiff and had such a political backing that his group formulated an astonishing and innovative proposal: elect their own pope. So Hippolytus became the first antipope in history, and Callixtus was the first to face such a recalcitrant challenger.

The main charge to Callixtus? He treated sinners too lightly. So Callixtus responded, "The Church is a place where the wheat and tares grow together." In 222, Callixtus was dead, and the Church elected a new pope: Pope Urban I. We don't know much about Urban other than he was disrupted by Hippolytus and his schismatic faction as well until he died in 230.

Urban I was succeeded by Pope Pontian, but early into his pontificate emerged the persecution of Emperor Maximus Thranx, focused on scattering or eliminating Christian leaders. Pontian went to the Sardinian mines. Realizing the Church needed its leaders to be with and among the people, Pontian decided to make another groundbreaking decision for a papacy: abdication. This decision, he figured, was what was best for the Church.

But a special individual went with Pontian to labor in the mines. Maximus Thranx had no use for discrimination in his persecution and ensured the leader of the divided Christians was sent to the mines as well: Hippolytus.

Much aghast at this turn of event, we are sure, the pope and the antipope worked for some years in strenuous labor, side-by-side. Whatever they particularly discussed is lost to history and we will never know. However, we do know that before the end, whatever Christian charity Pontian was able to display in the mines made a significant impression on the rebellious leader, and the two were reconciled. Hippolytus secured an order to disband the sect and to be reunited with the Church. Hippolytus, therefore, was also reconciled and became a saint. Through love and perseverance, the Church's first antipope controversy was resolved in short order, and the Church gained the invaluable theological insights of one of its best early-thinkers: St. Hippolytus.

Following the abdication of Pontian in 235, a new pope was elected, Anterus, a Greek. He died less than a year later.

Five popes in less than twenty years was not a bad figure for the early Church, but the Church was organized finally, somewhat publicly, and with antipopes and schismatic sects gaining ideas of their ability to control the future of the Church, stable and effective leadership was much in demand.

Fabian succeeded Anterus, and an important historian would happen to be at his ceremony. All were wondering about this choice for pontiff: would he last more than a year? Would he, too, be sent away to the mines? Might another schism break out? All present watched and wondered, when, as Eusebius records, a dove descended and landed on Fabian's head. An actual dove—the universal symbol of the

Holy Spirit—touched his brow and sat for a moment. Thus, everyone in attendance believed that Fabian was the correct choice.

In a few short years, the Church rediscovered the notion that love triumphs over evil and was given a pope who would remain in office for close to fifteen years.

Holy popes of the Early Church, pray for us.
St. Hippolytus, pray for us.

LIKE A SURGEON: ST. PHILIP NERI

By Shaun McAfee

In 1593, a Roman man was panicked when his wife suddenly fell ill. Her caretakers put her in a bed, and the local doctors made every attempt to bring her back to health. It was of no use—her health deteriorated so much that she couldn't move in any direction.

Worried and believing his bride was on her deathbed, he sought the only man in town who could work a miracle: Philip Neri (1515–1595).

"Philip, you must come! My wife is sick to the point of death!"

"Go away. She will be fine."

The man's hope increased, so he returned home. But the woman's health became worse as her body rejected every solid and liquid the staff attempted to feed her. She was undoubtedly on the brink of death, and her husband again returned to Philip.

"Nothing has gotten better as you said. She is much worse, and we fear this is the end for her. Please help!"

"Your wife will not die of this illness. She will recover her health as she was before. Go home."

"But—"

"Fine. I will follow you."

Philip followed the man, named Antonio Carracia. When they arrived at the man's house, the saint went up to the woman and asked, "Where does it hurt?" and she pointed.

Philip lightly touched that spot, pulled back his hand, and left. Before closing the door to the house, Philip reared his head to make eye contact with Antonio. "Be glad. You have nothing to fear," was all he said as he shut the door tightly. The woman was totally healed and in better health than before she became ill.

Upon receiving a victim in trauma, a skilled and trained surgeon will not lose focus, will not join the panic, and will not create a circus of fear. Philip Neri, a surgeon of souls, acted the same way, and for the same reason: worry and panic never make the situation better.

St. Philip Neri, pray for us.

A LAW-ABIDING CHRISTIAN: POPE ST. FELIX I

By Shaun McAfee

Towards the closing of the third century, Felix I came to the Chair of St. Peter and had the task of dealing with a progressively defiant bishop from Antioch.

The rebellious bishop was Paul of Samosata, who was deposed in a local synod to the satisfaction of the local faithful due to his unorthodox views of the Trinity. The people simply awaited the word from the pope on the findings of their synod.

Pope Felix sent a letter confirming proper Trinitarian theological views accepted by the Church, an affirmation of the synod's findings. Paul of Samosata was supposed to vacate his office but refused, even going so far as to hoard all the Church property he could gather in his home, which also belonged to the diocese.

The astute Antiochenes again wrote a letter to the pope, urging him to take up the matter with the law. The year was about 270, and it would be almost four decades until the Edict of Milan was to be signed, but the Church was growing in visibility and influence. In an act of sheer bravery, Pope Felix petitioned Emperor Aurelian. He replied, ordering all of the property to be returned back to the Roman Church.

Shrewd use of the law and unbridled bravery can accomplish much for Christians.

St. Felix I, pray for us.

"CREATOR OF HEAVEN AND EARTH": ST. PETER OF VERONA

By Shaun McAfee

Find it hard to write, read, or do anything when you have a massive headache? It's understandable, but it didn't keep one saint from delivering an important message.

Peter (1205–1252) was born in Verona 390 years before William Shakespeare would write his masterpieces *Romeo and Juliet* and *The Taming of the Shrew*, both of which took place in the northern Italy city of huge moats, walls, an arena dating to 70 BC, and highly influential civil and religious power in the area.

His parents were Cathars, adherents of a heresy involving denial of the created material world and a host of related beliefs involving reincarnation, ultra-strict dietary rules, and sexless marriages, among others. His uncle admonished him because of this when he heard him, at a very young age, recite the Apostles Creed paying particularly close attention to "Creator of heaven and earth."

Seeking an education in Bologna, he became a novice in the Dominican Order and was ordained sometime later.

He found himself preaching primarily in Lombardy, the beautiful foothills and lake country of such picturesque places as Como, Bellagio, Milan, Varese, Bergamo, and was highly reputed for his skill and wit in any argument.

Wit and skill invite envy, especially among those against whom it is employed, and the Dominican Order was formed for the chief purpose of putting a strict and swift end to the Albigensian heresy—the Cathars held a similar pattern of faith. Even though the Cathars denounced the killing of others, they found a loophole: hire an assassin.

Peter knew, and in a homily, he announced, "Let them do their worst. I shall be more powerful dead than alive."

The breakaway sect chose a man by the name of Carino from the commune of Balsamo. Hiding in a lowly place late at night on the road between Como and Milan, he waited with an accomplice for Peter and his brother companion.

Once their identity was confirmed, Carino paced forward and slammed his ax into the skull of Peter. As the accomplice chased down and mortally wounded the companion, Peter stood up, ax in scull, and wiped blood from his forehead in a calculated manner. With enough blood on his finger, he reached down to the ground and wrote a message to Carino: "I believe in God, the Father almighty, creator of heaven and earth." Then, he laid down and died.

His work was not completed. The message in a pool of blood must have made an impression on the assassin.

Carino stared down at the corpse with a head split wide open and the bloody words of the holy man. He then left his accomplice, walked straight to Forlì, and confessed to James Salomoni at the first Dominican convent he could find. Soon, and with great repentance, Carino entered the monastery and received the Dominican habit. Today, that same Carino is known as Blessed Carino of Balsamo.

The firm believer in the Apostles Creed since his first words, Peter of Verona was right: his greatest work as he had preached was accomplished when he was dead.

St. Peter of Verona, pray for us.

ST. BENEDICT DOES WHAT ST. BENEDICT DOES BEST

By Shaun McAfee

St. Benedict (480–547) came to destroy pagan temples and fight dragons—and he was all out of dragons. He was a likable priest, but sometimes success brings out envy in others. When this happened to a priest named Florentius, Benedict left Subiaco, the city where he had established a sizable community of monasteries. With his companions and a group of devoted monks, tradition tells us that he followed a divinely inspired path and arrived in the southern Italian commune of Cassino, around the year 529.

The host found the people of Cassino having returned to a mixture of Christian and pagan worship after a long period of decline in their town. The people there were in dire need of revival, inspiration, and faith. This, Benedict understood, would be the new project God had destined him to undertake.

On top of the hill overlooking lower Cassino remained an ancient temple to Jupiter and an altar to Apollo, joined by Roman guardian towers, pagan idols, a sacred grove, and a cyclopean wall.

Benedict climbed the mountain, surveyed the pagan site of worship, and left.

A short time later, he came back with tools of sledgehammers, and taking one huge lunge forward, he destroyed the pagan remains, obliterating the idols. When the dust settled, he set plans on converting the temple of Jupiter into a church dedicated to St. Martin of Tours, probably a hero of his since he was the founder of monasticism in France in the fourth century.

Benedict had the place totally wrecked and knew that since spiritual cancer had been removed, it was time to build new muscle and spiritual strength. So, in addition to ardent prayer, Benedict held hard work, including manual labor, in high regard and organized the monks in constructing the original structures of Monte Cassino, recycling many of the primitive slabs, columns, and other materials from the site and supplemented the build using the trees and other materials from the sacred grove on the hill.

Benedict performed a number of other miracles during and after the construction of the first Abbey of Monte Cassino, including what is considered his most important miracle: writing *The Rule of St. Benedict*. This abbey was his sacred home until his death in the mid sixth century. A bronze statue commemorating this moment can be seen in the garden, on the spot where the primitive oratory once stood.

When it comes to spiritual warfare, St. Benedict didn't mess around. It's not to say that we should commit vandalism and damage private property, but we should go to appropriate and necessary lengths to liberate the earth and its people from evil and false Gods.

St. Benedict of Nursia, pray for us.

ST. PHILIP NERI JOKES BEFORE, AND ABOUT, HIS DEATH

By Shaun McAfee

The saint from Florence was known for his madcap sense of humor. In moments of life when one would expect solemnity, Philip Neri (1515–1595) delivered full-out belly laugh moments. If it wasn't a knee-slapper, he at least used his wit to calm the room and give peace to his brethren. He held this reputation to the final hours of his life.

Eight days before he would die, a young disciple named Nero visited him on his recent recovery in health from an episode which saw him vomiting blood and convulsing. Expecting a warm thanksgiving, Nero was probably shocked when Philip told him, "I may have survived the disease of the moment, and feel well now, but my sons will not rejoice for long. The end of the conflict is near, and I shall die in such a manner that when it happens hardly anyone will know, they won't believe it when they hear it, and to begin with it will be just a rumor."

A day before his death, he told one of his closest companions, Pietro Consolini, to say Mass for him.

"Sure, I can say Mass tomorrow if you're not feeling well."

"No," Philip replied. "I need you to say a Mass for the dead."

Pietro smiled but didn't realize that Neri was referring to himself. He ushered himself away and prepared for further instructions. Neri, probably laughing in his head, let Pietro go with no further clarification. More deathbed humor would follow.

The next night, some of his followers gathered around him to observe his health and enjoy some time—perhaps their last, they suspected—with their spiritual father. Probably because his friends were moping about, Philip wanted them to go away but knew they would only be persuaded to leave if he could assure them of his health. But Neri, already annoyed with the excess attention, had to shoo them. To prove his cognition, he would tell them the time. Imagine their faces when, noting that the sun had set three hours earlier, he said, "Three hours, then if you add two onto that it makes five, if you add three, it makes six. Now off to bed with you!" I imagine that was his way of saying, "It's past your bed time." I also fancy he gave them a look that said, "You can pick your jaw up now."

You couldn't ask for a more joyful saint. His disciples loved him and stayed with him despite his numerous attempts to send them away. Bitterly crying as he prayed over them one final time, Philip Neri, the Third Apostle of Rome, died on the feast of Corpus Christi, just as it had been revealed to him ten days earlier.

Wit and humor are devices of charity and joy; there's sure holiness in an unpolluted and humble sense of humor.

St. Philip Neri, pray for us.

BE CAREFUL WHAT YOU PRAY FOR: ST. PHILIP NERI

By Shaun McAfee

Antonio Gallonio preserved a massive volume of stories about St. Philip Neri (1515–1595). Most of them are astonishing: he was almost continually predicting the future, fighting off demons, and caught in very interesting ecstasies. Throughout the biography of the saint, he tells the narrative of Neri's life, but now and then the reader gets to read about his wisdom.

Known as the Third Apostle of Rome, he brought the zeal of Catholicism back to the Eternal City by leading inner-city pilgrimages, overseeing construction of newer, bigger, and more spectacular churches, and more importantly, his nature and holiness changed the hearts of many lay people and clergy. But not everyone loved Philip—some clergy were particularly envious of him.

When he was celebrating Mass one day, he was in the middle of the consecration when he had an honest moment with God, saying, "Why is it, O good Jesus, that when I ask you so often, so earnestly, to give me the gift of patience, I am confronted with so many things that are liable to make me angry?"

He heard the inner voice of the Lord reply to him, "And why do you ask me for patience, Philip? I will strengthen you with patience, but my wish is for you to strive as hard as you can to acquire it, and I have given you these attacks to serve that purpose."

It happens that when we ask God to increase in us a virtue, he will give us ample opportunity to acquire it—but he won't do the work for us; we have to work at it.

St. Philip Neri, pray for us.

A BACKHANDED COMPLIMENT: ST. MACRINA THE YOUNGER

By Shaun McAfee

Macrina (329–379) came from a wealthy aristocrat family in Caesarea, Cappadocia, which is in present-day Turkey. She was named after her grandmother, also a saint, and was then after known as "the Younger." With the family name came the rich tradition of Christian charity. Her parents knew the spiritual value of a solid Christian upbringing and setting an example for piety by aiding the poor and encouraging persecuted Christians with funding and supplies.

Their influence and education rubbed off significantly on their children, and particularly in the spirituality and holiness of the eldest, Macrina. Already known for her piety, when her mother and father died, she took up a notably ascetic lifestyle—donating much of her wealth to the poor and the

Church, choosing to live in the same standards as the household laborers. She became a nun and set a great example for the rigors of the "Desert Mothers," visibly emphasizing the value of virginity as a reflection of the radiant purity of God.

The family names did not just pass to Macrina, but also to her brothers, Basil and Gregory, who would become Basil the Great and Gregory of Nyssa. The latter was the chief theologian who formed the Nicene Creed, and Basil was an ardent proponent of the Creed. Despite their skill in debate, elaborative philosophical lexicon, and acumen in ecclesial governance, sibling rivalry became evident when Gregory felt pressure from Rome when the emperor sided with the Arians, a heretical group that favored the theological denial of Jesus Christ as coequal and consubstantial with the Father. Clearly, Gregory needed the chastisement of an older sister to get his priorities in order.

She wrote a letter to her younger brother with a confusingly hilarious complement: "Will you not put an end to your failure to recognize the good things which come from God? Churches send you forth and call upon you as ally and reformer, and you do not see the grace in this? Do you not even realize the true cause of such great blessings, that your parents' prayers are lifting you on high, for you have little or no native capacity for this?"

Tactful or not, she was effective in her council: Gregory became one of the leading figures in the Early Church against Arianism at every level of influence and power. And it was, nobody can deny, all thanks to his older sister. Siblings, take note.

St. Macrina the Younger, pray for us.

ADVICE (AND A PRAYER) FOR NEWLYWEDS: ST. PHILIP NERI

By Shaun McAfee

Philip Neri (1515–1595) is often known as "the laughing saint," and it's for a good reason. When people least expected it, Philip would say, do, or share something hilarious.

That was the case when a fellow priest was preparing to join together a young couple in Holy Matrimony. Inexperienced and wanting to say something useful for the couple, he approached Neri.

"What do you think is the best prayer I can give to a newlywed couple?"

The priest replied immediately, "A prayer for peace."

St. Philip Neri, pray for us.

AFTER THE WELL:
ST. PHOTINA

By Shaun McAfee

The Roman Martyrology includes a special woman named Photina, and her story is kept and told by the Greeks.

After preaching the Gospel in many locations throughout the Middle East and Northern Africa, she found her way to Carthage. The ancient city east of what is now Tunis was ripe with Christians in the days of the Early Church. And typically, wherever the Faith went, there already stood the Romans, usually imprisoning Christians for the Faith. Photina was captured, imprisoned, and martyred with a group.

But she accomplished much before she died. She gave birth to sons, and one of them became St. Victor, the officer in the imperial army, governor in Gaul, and converter of St. Sebastian. Spanish Catholics pass on a story which tells that she preached to, converted, and baptized Domnina, daughter of Emperor Nero.

They were all brought to Rome by the emperor Nero around the same time, imprisoned, tortured brutally, and received the martyr's crown by being roasted over a slow fire, then flayed alive. Others were beheaded after equally horrible torture. Photina, though, seemed to be their spokesperson and for this received special attention, being brought before Nero himself after being kept in a well for days.

Nero asked Photina if she would now relent and offer sacrifice to the idols. Photina spit in the face of the emperor and, laughing at him, said, "O most impious of the blind, you profligate and stupid man! Do you think me so deluded that I would consent to renounce my Lord Christ and instead offer sacrifice to idols as blind as you?"

Hearing such words, Nero gave orders to again throw the martyr down the well again, where she surrendered her soul to God and died. This was around the year 66.

The most important detail from this saint's life is who she met before preaching the Gospel. The Roman Martyrology states that Photina was the Samaritan woman at the well who spoke with Jesus.

St. Photina, pray for us.

WHAT SHOULD WE DO WITH SAINT NARRATIVES THAT CONTAIN ERRORS OR INCONSISTENCIES?

By Shaun McAfee

If you were paying close attention, you noticed a few holes in the story of St. Photina. The gaping one is the placement of her son, Victor, with St. Sebastian in Gaul. Sebastian's story is world famous and his iconography is nearly everywhere. By the time Sebastian rose to fame, his life and martyrdom was corroborated by very influential, prolific, and trustworthy sources, particularly that of St. Ambrose of Milan. So all historians agree that he lived in the third century and died in the year 288.

That's more than two-and-a-half centuries after the story of the woman at the well in John's Gospel, making it impossible for her to have been the mother of a son who converted Sebastian in Gaul. And in the life of St. Sebastian, we don't read about a governor named Victor in his conversion.

But that doesn't make this entire story false: it simply suggests a warrant of due criticism in some of the details. And some of those details are spot on.

Again, the important detail is the timing. Nero, a matricidal emperor who assumed the role of the bride at his own wedding, was emperor until the year 68. His persecutions of Christians kicked off in 64 when three of the four districts in Rome were burned to the ground; he blamed the Christians, a small but influential sect, and many suspect he did this to hide himself as the cause of the fire.

Given the timing and the historical preservation of his anti-Christian and madman persona, it is highly likely that he would have persecuted Photina following this event. She, by that time, would be like Peter, nearing the end of her natural life. And having been rounded up from the known world and summoned to Rome to stand for her Faith and publicly mocked and executed was entirely probable because it is a narrative consistent with several others.

So, what should a reader or believer do with this story and others of similar substance? My advice is to cut out the obvious errors as legend. It's what Butler does in his *Lives of the Saints*, albeit in a less tactful way sometimes, but it's fair and reasonable treatment. Photina is probably the woman at the well, and we know that biblically, she preached to the Samaritans and probably went out from there after the Resurrection. We have no cause to discredit that. Her sons or companions might have been named Victor and Sebastian (or similar), and could have been mixed up with later stories upon telling and retelling—that sort of confusion is plentiful in the cases of the early saints. After cutting out the parts that are legend, retain the facts as facts, and treat the features that are probable or possible as just that: probable and possible. But don't discredit the entirety of the saint because of a few distracting details.

TUTOR TO THE TUDORS: BLESSED THOMAS ABEL

By Shaun McAfee

A man in the inner circle of the royal family went from chaplain, tutor, and friend to outlaw overnight for defending the marriage he helped foster. Thomas Abel (1497–1540) was a highly educated priest in England. He became a master of arts and received a doctorate of divinity from Oxford. He soon found himself as a personal tutor of the royal family and was a trusted advisor to many influential Catholics in London and surrounding areas.

So trusted was he that when Catherine of Aragon discovered her husband's plans to nullify the royal marriage, she made a plan with him: Thomas would deliver the king's errand to Emperor Charles V of Spain, requesting the marital dispensations of Pope Julius II. Secretly, though, she instructed him to explain to the emperor that the letter was created in order to discredit her marital claim and cause further injury to her.

Thomas Abel left, delivered the message, and returned with no papers—a success for the queen.

But that was the end of the streak of success, and his days of influencing others would change dramatically in becoming the central figure for public treatment of Catholics and those who would conspire against Henry VIII.

In a dramatic show of his faith and confidence in the indissolubility of Matrimony, he published *Invicta Veritas*, a treatise answering several opinions of those who supported the nullity efforts of Henry. It became a bestseller, perhaps because Henry VIII had all copies purchased and burned. Abel was immediately found and thrown into the Tower of London. On Christmas Eve, he was released but was seized once again and put in the Beauchamp tower in 1534.

This time, Henry suspected him of conspiring with Elizabeth Barton, a Catholic nun who did not silence her opinions of the crown. Once a highly supported figure and associate of Henry, she frequently prophesied against him and openly denounced his efforts of marrying Anne Boleyn.

Abel had little to do with the events of Barton's life, but his imprisonment went on, untried, for three more years. He made attempts to secure his release or affordances to celebrate Mass in his cell but was unsuccessful. Three more years went by before the glum and malnourished priest found an unlikely advocate: his jailor.

His keeper let him and some others arrested with him on "parole" but only to beg for alms. For this, the jailor was sent to the prison of Marshalsea, where the poorest of the city's offenders were kept. Anyone who gave alms to the prisoner priests was jailed with them. This included Bishop Richard Samson of Chichester.

That year, in 1540, he was summarily found guilty of the crime of "adhering to the Bishop of Rome," and read his sentence: "To be drawn on a hurdle to the place of execution, there to be hanged, cut down alive, your members to be cut off and cast in the fire, your bowels burnt before your eyes, your head smitten off, your body to be quartered at the king's will, and God have mercy on your soul."

He endured this martyrdom, as was common for the Catholic priest-martyrs of England under the treason legislation from 1534 to 1680. Pope Leo XIII beatified him and the other Fifty-Four English Martyrs in 1886.

Being a friend is easy. Being a friend when it's unpopular takes courage.

Blessed Thomas Abel, pray for us.

WHY ARE SOME CANONIZED QUICKLY WHILE OTHERS HAVE BEEN IN THE PROCESS FOR CENTURIES?

By Shaun McAfee

This is a question I'm sure every Catholic has asked themselves. There's no easy answer to it either, but I hope I can offer a few helpful thoughts and reasons.

That the Church possesses a process for giving a status to the heroes of our Faith is an interesting fact in itself. Catholics are not entirely unique: other sects and religions have similar honorifics for their historic ambassadors and champions. But the Catholic Church is without a doubt unparalleled in scale. We have more saints, older saints, and hold them in higher regard than any other religion—by far!

Unlike ancestor worship, we believe they still serve our mystical body. Unlike the practice of purely remembering their sacrifices, we believe their martyrdoms fertilize the soil of evangelized territories of the earth. Suffice it to say that the Catholic Church doesn't simply hold these heroes on pedestals: their lives and works and what we believe about them are truly different from the rest of the world.

Take a look at the history of the saints and the Church, though, and you'll notice there are some shifting points in history as to how we treat the saints and how they are included or referred to as "canonized."

It's important to remember that the word *canon* comes from the Greek *kanon*, which in its original usage denoted a straight rod, was later used for a measuring stick, and eventually came to mean a rule or norm. This is why we say that the Bible is our canon, because it is the finalized rule of Sacred Scripture. In AD 325, when the first ecumenical council of Nicaea was held, *kanon* started to obtain the restricted juridical denotation of a law promulgated by a synod or ecumenical council, as well as that of an individual bishop. Think of Canon Law, or when a priest is known as a canon—they are each similar usages of the word.

It is that norm of recognizing an individual as a saint that has matured since the infant days of the Church. Recall from other reading in this book that, early on, few rules for canonization were enforced if in use—and those rules were not universal because much regulatory liberty was granted to the local bishop. Therefore, through the centuries of the

Church, we notice a maturing of the rules and processes of canonization from local initiatives to petitions to the Holy See. As those rules and processes changed, perhaps (we cannot be completely sure), the causes were delayed, slowed, or postponed.

That's one thought, and along with it is the implied reality that canonized saints require a petition, which means that the responsibility of canonization falls on the living faithful—not solely on the curial shepherds of the Church or the pope. Producing adequate content for evaluation of a person's life to start and, more importantly, to continue the cause of a saint is one that requires unremitting enterprise. Perhaps—in speculation—some of these causes have not enjoyed the continuity of labor they deserved.

Here's another idea I have about those who have remained in an open cause for many years. The Church is like a factory for holy people. There are, first of all, a huge amount of causes still open at the Holy See. One glance at the feasts and memorials on the calendar of saints and one will quickly realize there are numerous blessed on that calendar too, to say nothing of the many venerables and servants of God. Certainly to attain any of these levels of public recognition is a testament to an individual's love for God and neighbor.

As for the process, only speculation can answer the question of the relation between time and cause for different saints. In any case, we should drop to our knees and praise God—the Church produces an incalculable amount of holiness in the lives of the faithful!

THREE COUNTER-
REFORMERS CONVERGE

By Shaun McAfee

It is an understatement to say that Robert Bellarmine (1542–1621) was a prominent figure in the Counter-Reformation. In matters of apologetics, Robert *was* the Counter-Reformation. Any Catholic that held hopes of undertaking the work of debating a Protestant simply had to read the work of Bellarmine. Because not only did he understand Protestant theology, he argued persuasive disputes on the most complex and confusing religious jargon of the time.

He rigorously took up the study of Hebrew in order to better gain insight on the original meaning of Old Testament Scripture and continued similar studies in New Testament Greek. Bellarmine laid a foundation for Catholic apologetics that still exists today: he was the very first to use a combination of the Scriptures, the Early Church Fathers, ecumenical councils, and Church history to form arguments. He stopped at nothing to address every morsel of heresy and dogma, writing the three volumes of *The Controversies*, composing over nine million words in defense of the Catholic faith.

Naturally, and as expected, all of this led to greater popularity and demand for Father Bellarmine. It must be understood that although Robert's time in the Church was one of controversy and trouble, it was a period that cultivated many saints. These saints sometimes had interactions, with interesting stories to boot!

While in Louvain, the lives of Bellarmine, Philip Neri, and the very influential Charles Borromeo (1538–1584) converged. Charles was busy with correcting the insatiably corrupt city of Milan. And was in great need, at least to him, of an orator to preach against the stifling heresies. He would settle for no less than his own choice priests. He wrote Philip Neri in Rome, who ignored him. Then he began to pester Neri. Philip wrote a lovely note in return:

> You accuse me of not being mortified because I will
> not let you have Father Baronius, but I am certain, and
> by your leave I am going to tell you so frankly, that
> you are far more lacking in detachment. Many people,
> including the bishops of Rimini and Vercelli, say this
> about you, and also that you are not above downright
> robbery. When you set eyes on a capable man, you
> immediately try to allure him to Milan. You are a most
> daring and audacious robber of holy and learned men.

As the proverb said, you despoil one altar in order to adorn another.

Neri did not hold back. Caesar Baronius succeeded Neri as the superior of the Oratory.

Charles set his eyes on Bellarmine, playing the same card with the Jesuits. Father Adorno, still in a position of Jesuit power, abetted the efforts of Borromeo but was unsuccessful. Louvain was to keep Bellarmine for another short while until 1576. Robert would return to Italy to begin a work that reshaped how the Catholic Church trained priests, becoming the Chair of Controversies of the pontifical Roman College, a position and curriculum created specifically for Bellarmine.

Whatever Cardinal Borromeo was, he was not wrong about his judgment. Everyone he ever set his eyes on or mentored personally did something spectacular for the Church. There's an art to professional confrontation. Neri and Borrmeo did not retaliate against one another. They both kept their eyes on the same goal: to reform and re-evangelize the Church. And between the three of them, Bellarmine, Borromeo, and Neri, and a few of their friends, did just that.

Saints of the Counter-Reformation, pray for us.

ST. CATHERINE LABOURÉ AND THE MIRACULOUS MEDAL

By Laura Hensley

"Sister Labouré! Sister Labouré! Sister Labouré!"

Finally, Catherine (1806–1876) awoke to the sound of a child calling her name. This was very strange, since it was the middle of the night and dark, except for a lit candle held by the child calling her name. This was the night of July 18, 1830.

Fully awake, she heard the child then say, "Come to the chapel. The Blessed Virgin awaits you."

Catherine quickly arose, got dressed in her novice Sister of Charity habit, and followed the mysterious child to the chapel. When she got there, she knelt and waited for what seemed several minutes. She was worried someone would catch her in the chapel so late at night.

The child announced, "Here is the Blessed Virgin." She heard the rustling of silk as Mary walked down the altar stairs and sat in the director's chair. Catherine doubted a moment this was Mary, rather just a dream, when the child said, "This is the Blessed Virgin." Immediately, she believed and threw herself on Our Lady's knee with her hands rested upon her lap.

Mary explained to Catherine that God has a mission for her but warned her of the great difficulties and torments she would have to overcome. Most importantly, she must always "recognize at all times what God wanted of her." As Mary spoke, Catherine would ask questions and Mary would respond. This was a conversation just like a mother and daughter would have, spending over two hours together!

Catherine listened intently as Mary explained that she could only tell the one in charge of her about the vision, who was Father Aladel. And she did.

A week later, the sufferings that Mary told her that would affect France, its leaders, and the archbishop began. Mary assured her the Vincentian Fathers and the Sisters of Charity would be spared from this persecution. For Catherine, this was grim proof that what she experienced wasn't a delusion and that God would ask her to fulfil a great mission, though she still did not know what that mission would be. Fr. Aladel also had to discern if Catherine had actually received this vision as she said she had, and this was just the first proof that this could be true.

On November 27, 1830, while praying with the other sisters in the chapel at 5:30 in the evening, she once again heard the rustling of silk, just as she had that early morning when Our Lady first appeared. Then, a beautiful vision appeared before Catherine. After seeing the first image, Catherine heard Mary say, "Have a medal struck after this model. All who wear it will receive great graces; they should wear it around the neck. Graces will abound for persons who wear it with confidence." Then, the image turned and she was shown what was to be the back side of the medal. Then it was gone. None of the other sisters saw or heard anything. These were the only visions she had, but she continued to speak with Mary in her prayers.

Catherine shared the second vision and mission to Fr. Aladel, but he refused to help her create the medal. Catherine kept seeing the same images, which gave her strength to go back again, and again, yet the priest sternly refused to strike the medal.

Catherine, although frustrated, was always obedient when Fr. Aladel refused her, but the repeated visions told her that she should not give up. She realized this was part of the suffering Mary told her she would have to accept.

Fr. Aladel, in goodwill and good faith, had to be 100 percent sure what Sister Catherine was saying was truly from Mary and God. Catherine kept her vow to Mary to not tell anyone and remain anonymous; therefore, the weight of what Fr. Aladel was being asked to do would fall solely upon his shoulders. Ultimately, Fr. Aladel and Catherine kept this secret for forty-six years, no doubt, a small miracle and act of humility in itself.

In 1832, the medal was designed and accepted by Fr. Aladel. He initially ordered twenty thousand medals, originally known as the "Medal of the Immaculate Conception."

The first group of medals were distributed quickly, and immediately, stories of miracles were shared by those who wore the medal. By 1836, several million had been created, and people instead gave it its more popular name: the "Miraculous Medal." Besides the rosary, it has become the widest distributed sacramental in the Catholic world.

A lesson anyone can take away from the story of St. Catherine Labouré and the Miraculous Medal is to endure in obedience. The more difficult lesson is to trust, also, the virtue of prudence. Fr. Aladel's merit is as deserving of our contemplation, because he possessed and employed a virtuous skepticism—not to doubt the Lord's eminent visions and miracles, but in being patient, and piously testing, in order to confirm the will of God. Surely, it would be great to be the priest that immediately said "Yes!" but unfathomably difficult to be the priest charged with solving this mystery with little more than a testimony. We have lessons to learn from them both.

St. Catherine Labouré, pray for us.

ST. FAUSTINA AND THE
IMAGE OF DIVINE MERCY

By Laura Hensley

Sister Faustina Kowalska (1905–1938) was in her cell on the evening of February 22, 1931, when she saw the most beautiful vision. It was of our Lord Jesus holding his upright hand in a blessing and pointing with his left to his Divine Heart with rays of light pouring out, one red and one pale.

The vision gave her great joy when she heard Jesus say, "Paint an image according to the pattern you see, with the signature: Jesus, I trust in You. I desire that this image be venerated, first in your chapel and throughout the world. I promise that the soul that will venerate this image will not perish. I also promise victory over enemies already here on earth, especially at the hour of death. I Myself will defend it as My own glory."

After the vision, she told her confessor what she had seen and that Jesus asked her to paint the image. Concerned, the priest dismissed her vision and reasoned that her vision was misinterpreted: Jesus meant he wanted the image painted into her soul.

Immediately as she left the confessional, she heard Jesus say, "My image is already in your soul. I desire that there be a Feast of Mercy. I want this image, which you will paint with a brush, to be solemnly blessed on the first Sunday after Easter; that Sunday is to be the Feast of Mercy."

Faustina was troubled by this mission and spoke with her Mother Superior about it. She told Kowalska to ask for a clear sign that this was from Jesus. Soon and sure, as Faustina prayed, Jesus told her the sign would be clear through the graces given through the image.

Even with this reassurance, she prayed for the task to be taken from her. When she brought the issue to the attention of Father Andrasz, her priest, he said, "I will dispense you from nothing, Sister; it is not right for you to turn away from these interior inspirations, but you must absolutely—and I say, absolutely—speak about them to your confessor; otherwise you will go astray despite the great graces you are receiving from God."

More than a year passed by and Faustina neglected to paint the image. One evening in adoration, she received another vision of the Lord saying to her, "Know that if you neglect the matter of the painting of the image and the whole work of mercy, you will have to answer for a multitude of souls on the day of judgement." These words filled her soul with fear and anguish. Unable to paint herself, she asked Jesus for "visible help" to accomplish this mission. Jesus assured Faustina of the help she would receive.

On May 25, 1933, she was sent to Vilnius in Lithuania and given Father Sopocko as her spiritual director. On this day, she heard the voice of Jesus say, "This is the visible help for you on earth. He will help you carry out My will on earth." Even though Jesus pointed out this priest as the one who would help her, she still held back for a time. This caused her great anxiety and distress, until finally she poured out her soul to him.

Father Sopocko knew of a local artist, Eugene Kazimirowski, and from January 2, 1934 on, he met with Faustina several times to get a detailed description of the image that was to be painted. After giving the artist adequate time, she went to view the painting and was greatly disappointed because the image of Jesus wasn't anything close to the beauty she had met in her vision.

She didn't want to hurt Kazimirowski's feelings and kept it inside until she finally was able to weep in the chapel. As she prayed, "Who will paint you as beautiful as you are to me?" the Lord answered, "Not in the beauty of the color, nor the brush lies the greatness of this image, but in My grace." Jesus also told her, "My gaze from this image is like My gaze from the cross."

The image was not displayed in a church until the Sunday after Easter at the Mother of Mercy shrine in 1936 and finally hung in 1937 in St. Michael's Church in Vilnius. During World War II, the image was hidden so it was not stolen by the Nazis. Adolph Hylo painted the second image of Divine Mercy in 1943. The original image was moved and hidden several times, finally ending up in a church near the Russian border. In 1970, the Russians ransacked the church, but they miraculously left the Divine Image. In 1986, a parish priest snuck the image back to Vilnius. Finally, on April 30, 2000, Pope St. John Paul II canonized Blessed Maria Faustina Kowalska and established the Sunday after Easter as Divine Mercy Sunday.

Faustina's diary relates the rays of light within the image to life and salvation, stating, "The two rays denote blood and water. The pale ray stands for the water which makes souls righteous. The red ray stands for the blood which is the life of souls."

Faustina persisted in trusting God, though counting herself unable and unworthy. It is the Mercy of God that proves her right.

St. Faustina, pray for us.

HOPE FOR THE SEX ADDICT: ST. AUGUSTINE

By Mike Panlilio

Augustine was the bishop of Hippo in the fourth and fifth centuries, and he lived a life that was full of surprises—for himself and the people who knew him.

Before his conversion, Augustine was definitely the bad boy wherever he went, living like a wild animal with regard to lust.

So wild was his lust that he ended up with a child out of wedlock. That didn't stop him, as he lived with a mistress for a near-decade. In his autobiography, *Confessions*, we find out that the mistress was the mother of his baby. Furthermore, St. Augustine took in another mistress after the first left him for his disinterest in marriage.

Also in his *Confessions*, Augustine wrote about his life as a sex addict: "Because my will was perverse it changed to lust, and lust yielded to become habit, and habit not resisted became necessity." The word *necessity* is key here. Humans do not "need" sex to live—look at celibate religious men and women. But Augustine had such a dependence on sex that he considered it, at some point, a necessity.

In time and with Augustine's cooperation, God was able to give the future saint the grace to leave behind the life of lust and was able to continue in a life of celibacy! This is good news because if God can work on St. Augustine, then there's hope for everyone who has any amount (or form) of sex addiction.

What's odd about the life of Augustine is that he was able to have a high position of authority (and influence) in the Catholic Church, despite his sexual past. Outside of the Church, you normally need to have a "clean" past in order to be in positions of authority, but God's ways are not man's ways. If we repent of our sins and are transformed, God can lead us to a great life and hope is never lost.

St. Augustine, pray for us.

THE TIME ST. NICHOLAS SLAPPED A HERETIC

By Maggie Van Sciver

"The giver of every good and perfect gift has called upon us to mimic his giving, by grace, through faith, and this is not of ourselves." So said Nicholas (270–343), bishop of Myra (modern-day Turkey), in the fourth century.

However well Nicholas desired to cooperate with that grace, it is said that all fall short of the glory of God, and the saint who would bless the season of Christmas was not exempt from the snare of temptation. Although many other tales of his life feature demonstrations of giving Christ-like gifts, one gift in particular doled out to the heretic, Arius, at the Council of Nicaea was, on the surface, less than an imitation of Christ's perfect love and mercy—or was it justice?

This gift came to Arius who proposed the error that the nature of Jesus was not divine nor was he an equal member of the Trinity. Arius reasoned that this was because the Son was created, not begotten.

In a dramatic gesture, Nicholas, who could no longer contain his frustration at the continued belligerence and recalcitrance of Arius, rebuked his fellow bishop with not only strong words but a slap to the cheek, according to ancient traditions. Whether a slap, or a punch, his motive was not intended to inflict pain but rather to knock Arius back to his senses and away from the heresy he was spewing.

His actions did not go unnoticed: Nicholas was stripped of his bishop's garments for his outburst—a milder punishment than his hand being cut off, which would have been the punishment he earned for such an act in Nicaea of the fourth century. Nicholas was also thrown into prison for his impetuous outburst. Later records of these events say Christ and his holy mother appeared to Nicholas while in prison, clothing him in rich vestments and astounding his jailers when they saw him the next day. Nevertheless, Nicholas was served a very brief sentence, and Emperor Constantine, who had assembled the Council of Nicaea, even apologized for his sentence.

At first glance, the actions of Nicholas seem hot-headed and downright sinful. *How can a Christian bishop lose his temper?* It's simple to form similar conclusions, but there appears to be room for a holy storming. After all, did Christ not turn over tables in the temple when it became a place for worldly interactions instead of heavenly?

If we see the strike made by Nicholas not delivered as a physical misapplication but as a symbolic gesture to rebuke Arius's disobedience, it serves as a punctuation mark on the verbal rebuke Nicholas delivered to Arius, reaffirming Christ's divinity and place within the Holy Trinity. Ultimately, the area of Myra never fell prey to the heresy of Arianism, and this could be attributed to Nicholas's strong defense of the truth and the stand he took when confronted with Arius in person.

We have to ask ourselves: are we, too, outraged by heresy?

St. Nicholas of Myra, pray for us!

SAY THIS FIVE TIMES FAST—SAINTS SUFFER IN SECRET: BLESSED MIGUEL PRO

By Maggie Van Sciver

Laughter erupted from the group standing around the young priest. The joke he had told wasn't remarkably witty or endearingly slapstick, but the laughter was continually renewed as the group witnessed the man's exuberance at his own wisecrack. Just when it seemed his hilarity was subsiding, he would bend over clutching his sides once more, or wipe tears from the corners of his eyes, gasping for breath. Who cannot but laugh with contagious mirth?

This newly-ordained priest, Fr. Miguel Pro S.J. (1891–1927), would later earn renown as one of Mexico's great martyrs during the persecution of the Faith that took place in the first half of the twentieth century. At his death, his voice rang out in faith and courage in a way that shook the world—but the exclamation that rang out from his diaphragm on that day in 1927 was, in truth, simply the more audible echo of a multitude of hidden sacrifices and acts of love carried out on behalf of Christ, his King.

Fr. Miguel's propensity for humor in all forms, but especially the kind of jokes that made him bend over and slap his knee, was really just a cover-up on his part. He suffered from a chronic stomach ailment that caused him a great deal of pain. The condition worsened while he was completing seminary in Belgium in 1925, where he, along with other priests, had fled to continue their studies.

Multiple surgeries to resolve the condition were unsuccessful, so Fr. Miguel offered up the ulcerous pain as a sacrifice to God. He had developed the habit of telling jokes when he felt particularly intense bouts of pain in order to clutch his sides and bend over so others remained unaware of his suffering.

Nonetheless, Fr. Miguel's superiors were aware of his condition and reluctant to allow him to return to his persecuted homeland. However, he was insistent that the suffering Church in Mexico needed priests to administer the sacraments. His years of consistently offering small sacrifices throughout the day no doubt prepared him to make the ultimate sacrifice of his own life.

Miguel once wrote in a letter that "[I] sigh to go to heaven and start tossing off arpeggios on the guitar with my guardian angel." Perhaps after his glorious martyrdom, in his perfect joy, he took a break to bend over and laugh once more, clutching his sides to see the defiant Mexican people line the street in thousands to mourn his death and celebrate the Faith in direct defiance to the president's outlawing of public demonstrations.

Blessed Miguel Pro, pray for us! And Viva Cristo Rey!

SILENCE IS A STRATEGY: ELIZABETH LESEUR

By Maggie Van Sciver

E lisabeth Leseur (1866–1914) was an accomplished French woman living in Paris at the turn of the twentieth century. Her Catholic upbringing involved her in a wide variety of social circles in Paris. She met her husband, Felix, when they were both in their early twenties, and they were married two years later.

Felix, an intellectual who travelled in prestigious circles, had been raised Catholic but fell away from the Faith during his higher education. His promise to Elisabeth was to respect his bride's religious convictions, and he did so for a brief time into their twenty-five-year marriage, but his atheistic inclinations soon surfaced, and he began to persecute her.

To flex his intellectual muscles, Felix accumulated a vast library of anti-Catholic literature, which he forced Elisabeth to read. Their social circles were purposefully made up of people who held the same beliefs as Felix, and this isolated her from the influence from, or semblance of, a Catholic culture. He went further, constructing obstacles to her practice of the Faith, including being adamant that they serve meat on Fridays to guests.

Felix later admitted that he sought to destroy her faith outright, a feat which he nearly accomplished eight years into their marriage. He had increasingly pressured her so that for a period she abandoned the practice of the Catholic faith. He wrote that he intended to lead her to liberal Protestantism as a steppingstone to radical agnosticism. By the grace of God, Elisabeth's eyes were opened to the lack of substance and truth contained in the books he pressed upon her and she experienced a powerful return to Catholicism.

Elisabeth and Felix, though fundamentally at odds in their beliefs, had a loving marriage otherwise and continued to travel throughout Europe and enjoyed entertaining friends and family in Paris and at their summer residence. They even made religious pilgrimages together, including to Rome, where Elisabeth consecrated her life to God, and to Lourdes, where she went in thanksgiving for the successful removal of a cancerous tumor. Felix willingly made these pilgrimages in order to further cement his own skepticism but admitted he was at times moved by her devotion.

The pace of travelling and entertaining for the Leseurs decelerated as Elisabeth experienced bouts of ill-health. She had been prone to illness since childhood due to increasing problems with her liver, and finally cancer signaled her decline. During her final years, Felix's heart softened as he witnessed the joy and comfort her faith brought his wife even as she was bedridden and experiencing great pain. He observed the steady flow of visitors to whom Elisabeth seemed to be a spiritual mentor. Elisabeth's disposition remained ever cheerful and patient even as her suffering increased, and it was only in the concluding months of her life that Felix heard her cry out during bouts of pain, "My God, have pity on us; on me

Elisabeth died in Felix's arms in 1914. Although they enjoyed a loving marriage, it was only now that Felix discovered the whole depth of his wife's rich interior life. He witnessed the multitude of mourners, some of whom he had never even seen before, but whom Elisabeth's work and spirituality had deeply impacted.

One day, he found a letter that she had written to him, perhaps knowing he would read it only after she was gone. Inside, she laid out directions for after her death: a very simple funeral, requests for Masses to be said frequently in the days and years following, as well as requests for her husband to continue her charitable work and look after her remaining relatives. In her letter, she wrote confidently of Felix's return to the Catholic faith. This brought to mind for Felix predictions she had made before her death: "When I am dead, you will be converted; and when you are converted, you will become a religious."

Still dismissive, Felix resolved to make a journey to the recently popularized site of the Lourdes grotto to prove the rumors there as fake. He found himself deeply challenged, though, as he related the patient silence in Elisabeth's life and that of St. Bernadette. Their silent testimony became deafening witnesses to his need for interior change, and at the Lourdes grotto, he experienced a full and permanent conversion to the Catholic faith.

The letter was just the beginning, as Felix discovered more of Elisabeth's writings, and in discovering what was hidden from him, seeing that every suffering she had experienced was offered for his conversion. Through her incredible witness of charity and holy patience, more scales fell from his eyes. He realized in her cries, she had been offering those pains for *his* soul.

Elisabeth's deep, steadfast faith, even in the midst of isolation and suffering, inspired Felix's return to the Catholic Church. Felix became a Dominican and was ordained a priest in 1923. He published her diary in 1917 and opened the cause for her canonization in 1934, and from the time of his ordination until the Second World War, he travelled around, speaking about her apostolate and disposition. Perhaps no one is a better witness to the redemptive power of suffering when united with the Will of God as Felix.

Although she is not yet a canonized saint, there is an active and strong cause for her canonization established in 1934, designating her currently a Servant of God. Her life shows us that sometimes, silence is the best strategy for evangelization.

Servant of God Elisabeth Leseur, pray for us.

CAN I BECOME A SAINT?

By Shaun McAfee

Yes. Anyone can become a saint, but it is that idea of becoming one that is critical to understand.

In some translations of the Bible, such as the RSVCE, Philippians 1:1 has Paul referring to living Christians as "saints." He says, "To all the saints in Christ Jesus who are at Philippi, with the bishops and deacons: Grace to you and peace from God our Father and the Lord Jesus Christ" (1–2). When he says *saints*, he is meaning holy people who belong to God.

Oftentimes, we make the mistake of forgetting that the saints are not just those who have lived glorious and famous lives and performed amazing miracles but those who were pious and saintly in secret too. It's good to be a saint on earth, but our supreme goal should be our residence in heaven. Allowing ourselves to live in cooperation with the free graces, to make frequent use of the sacraments, to avoid sin, and have true regret for those sins we have committed are the straightforward instructions we have to becoming saints.

I recommend tossing out the egotistical idea of being canonized but to live every day with the knowledge that God is watching, building your room in his house, and building your reward as you build your merit through self-sacrifice and loving others. *Become* a saint by living every day with a single goal in mind—getting to heaven—because nothing else matters. That's the only way to sainthood with which we should be concerned.

CONTRIBUTORS

Alex R. Hey is an ADHD coach and the founder of Reset ADHD.com. He lives in South Dakota, and his writing has been published by local papers, EpicPew.com, and TheBat manUniverse.net. Alex is the author of *Eugène de Mazenod: A Saint for Today* which comes highly recommended by his mother.

Brooke Gregory is a freelance writer, editor, and consultant. She holds a BA in religion from Flagler College, is currently pursuing her MS in mental health counseling, and hopes to focus her career on serving the terminally ill and their loved ones. She is a prior contributor at EpicPew.com.

Jessica McAfee is a co-author of *Inseparable: Five Perspectives on Sex, Life, and Love in Defense of Humanae Vitae* (Catholic Answers, 2018). She is a stay-at-home mother of four.

Laura Hensley is a wife, stay-at-home mother of four, and lives by the philosophy of God, Family, and Country. She contributes to EpicPew.com.

Maggie Van Sciver grew up in Indiana and Colorado and is a military spouse currently living in Vicenza, Italy with her husband and daughter, where she enjoys traveling and adding to her ever-growing recipe stack.

Deacon Marty McIndoe converted to Catholicism from the Methodist Church in 1973 and was in the first class of deacons for the Diocese of Rockville Centre on Long Island, NY, ordained on October 4, 1980. He has served the diocese as a member of the Long Island Charismatic Service team and he has written for several publications, including EpicPew.com. He is Chaplain for The St. Joseph Prater Center in Patchogue as well as for AOH Division Five, HALO Missions, and Teams of Our Lady. He belongs to the Society of Franciscan Deacons (TOR) of Rockville Centre. He blogs at www.deaconmarty.com.

Mike Panlilio currently works as Coordinator of Religious Education at the Marine Corps Base in Quantico, Virginia. Previously, Mike has also worked as Director of Religious Education and Youth Ministry in the Arlington Diocese. He is a Lay Dominican, contributes to Epicpew.com, leads a local Catholic book club, and lives in Falls Church, Virginia.

Sarah Spittler is a graduate of the University of Notre Dame and a prior contributor at EpicPew.com.

Theresa Zoe Williams received her BA in Theology, Catechetics and Youth Ministry, and English Writing from Franciscan University of Steubenville. She currently lives with her husband and children in Colorado.

ABOUT THE AUTHOR

Shaun McAfee is a convert to the Catholic faith, and his inspiring story has been told in numerous places, including The Coming Home Network International's *The Journey Home*. He is the author of *I'm Catholic: Now What?* (Our Sunday Visitor, 2019), *20 Answers: Conversion* (Catholic Answers, 2019), *Social Media Magisterium* (En Route, 2018), *Reform Yourself!* (Catholic Answers Press, 2017), and *Filling Our Father's House* (Sophia Press, 2015), among several other titles. He is the founder and editor of EpicPew. com, blogs at the *National Catholic Register*, writes for *Catholic Answers Magazine*, and has written for numerous Catholic resources. Shaun earned a Master of Dogmatic Theology from Holy Apostles College and Seminary. He currently lives in Vicenza, Italy with his wife, Jessica, and four kids, Gabriel, Tristan, Dominic, and Alette.